I0157765

Cover Design by Osman Bah.

ISBN 978-0-615-56790-7

LOOKING THROUGH THE I:
AN EXISTENTIAL PHILOSOPHY

By:
Timothy M. Cradle

Baltimore, MD 21225

Dedicated to my mother,
Lynette,
And to my sister
Stacie.
For a lifetime of conversations.

CONTENTS

PREFACE

We come to a time in which it is taken for granted that we enjoy the greatest heights of individual freedom. And as with anything that is taken for granted we forget the value and indeed the nature of this situation. There were times in history when the nature of individual liberty had no meaning. A person was a commodity, as the serf, the slave, the vassal; in other words an appendage of the power to be. We come today of the reversal the person's relationship to the social structure, and in the process we have overlooked the collective nature of society, thinking that it disrupts our liberty. It is hard to move from this conceptualization, when there are many who argue for a libertarian utopia with logic that begs examination. Yet there is no examination, because the argument is posed in ways where what is on the surface seem to make up the entirety of the reasoning. It is in a word simple. Then it is important for us to examine this contemporary individual, the way that we make arguments and the self as such. This is what it means to look through – analyze – what it means to be an I – an individual.

PART ONE

INDIVIDUALISM

Anything that exists only exists by the qualities that define it. In matters subjective these qualities are malleable, and the characteristics thus attributed today may be wholly irrelevant even a year from today. With that said the characteristics themselves never change. The immutable character of being an individual never changes; as one person the unit of measurement will always be the individual. Individualism is not however the exercise of being an individual. One can only be an individual by being counted as one person from a multitude.

To embody individualism you must take some overt steps against your own socialization. Cohesive man, or society, is not the anti-individual indeed it is the support system for individual man. It is individualist man who seeks to take advantage of individual man as cohesive man or I should say collected man. The reality of this condition is not an exaggeration; a certain percentage of man will be antisocial and antagonistic. A great deal will have been accomplished to reduce their number. And although individualism is a reality it is not a necessity, one can be a fully realized individual while living as part of and indeed for the greater cohesive of mankind. We have met the enemy here and he is us.

The incessant malady then, which presents itself today, is the removal of individual man from cohesive mankind and the placing of this individual as antagonist to broader society. I do not intend to imply that the respect for individual man, the recognition of his own thoughts and predilections as paramount to his own domain of influence, is misplaced.

What I mean to convey is the lack of a sense of responsibility to the next person. Individualism should have a bad name, but today it has transcended its traditional bonding to egotism, and cupidity; those aspects which drive the individualist.

It perhaps seems natural that man functions in that ascribed mode, yet nothing about our cohesive civilization as society suggest that it is indeed an aspect of the human being. There is a vanity and luxury that goes with individualism that goes beyond the normal form and function of a society. This is typically described as human progress, however if it is progress why do we not find a way for all persons to enjoy this advancement rather than exploiting the advancement for a temporal advantage.

Individualism is only agreeable when it is the support of individual ends, which do not exclude or exploit cohesive means. I cannot then have anything more than a skeptic's view of individualism as an ethos for people to embody.

The individualist functions as something apart from society, and confuses what they would consider as uniqueness with their acquisitiveness. And how can one achieve the greatest heights of acquisitiveness? By separating themselves from a unit of the mass, to outside of the mass, and looking at the mass as a resource.

The individualist creates a "them" to be exploited as consumer and producer, to be moved aside indifferently or utterly crushed more like an enemy and less like subtle competition. Once the "them" is created, and the individualist realizes that there are other individualist entities it transforms the interexchange to an "us versus them" exchange where the "them" becomes any group of persons athwart the individualist greatest desires.

Although this is fundamentally anti-social behavior, the behavior is not classed as such. This is because there is not an abjuration from socialization, even though there is action that actively harms society in that it alters the way in which socialization occurs.

The social structures that bond a society together are everywhere besieged by the function of individualism. As we are all individuals it is not difficult for the individualist strain to appeal to that aspect of our existence, and in creating the confusion of the individual with the individualist.

This appeal can convince the most thoughtful persons to exist counter to their own interest and supportive of the interests of the individualist. More of the "them" turned into the "us". This is exploitation. The individualist must exploit to ratify their profligate standing. Exploitation does not have to be a euphemism, if I rephrase it as take advantage of, contract with, or hire, it will convey more closely what I mean to say.

If the individualist does not seek to exploit the individual then they will not be able to create anything for them self - there is no such organization that can be run on a large scale by one person alone. They need the individual; the individual however does not need the individualist, as the individual can derive from society what they need to subsist.

As mental deformity is natural, so too is individualism, or at least that is so on the surface. In reality it is artifice and there is a strong aspect of individualism that is alike the most dangerous of criminals in society. That prevalent aspect is that of anti-socialism. We think of the serial murderer as fundamentally anti-social, however when we consider the seemingly benign actions in society that harm people we hesitate to label them anti-social.

Anything is anti-social when it is harmful to the greater society or nature; this can include the misdistribution of material wealth, the destruction of natural resources and environment, the eminent domain of the state, and many more instances of a like nature.

It seems that only in man is individualism a really existing condition. There are many animals that live individually, and only seem comparable to human individualists when they take food or territory from other animals. So I can only reason individualism as a human defect.

Anti-social behavior is that which lacks regard for and recognition of others as having a similar value and has the potential to damage society. Individualism takes the individual out of society and forces them to reflect on society, but not with noble aims, more likely with aims to direct society in a way that conforms to their voracity. If an individual steals away from society to promote humanist enterprise then they are pro social and although equally exploitative of their role they are rendered necessary by the latter's existence.

There must by necessity exist a Churchill for every Hitler; the dismay of course is that Hitler does not need to exist in the first place, Germany would have obviously been better off had he stuck to painting. Beyond that, Churchill is not the objectively honorable man that history proffers in quotations and pictorials. Anti-social behavior and individualism are synonymous if not symptoms of one or the other.

Introverted and anti-social behavior has been un-intentionally drawn together though neither is the same, nor do they act the same in their relating of an introvert to society and an anti-social person to society. An introvert can most simply be described as a shy person, concerned principally with their own sphere.

Of course an introvert can be individualist, but these are not necessarily linked. The introvert withdraws from socializing, the anti-social person harasses society, and the individualist exploits society. The difference in the anti-social person and the individualist is only the intent, the nature or function is the same.

In the animal we do see many instances of acting individually, though there are many more that exhibit a collectivist nature. The pack, the herd, the flock, this mode of socialization is where we see the non-human animal as it relates to nature. It is the individual piece of a cooperative clique, and needs to be so for its means of survival. This is not unlike the way mankind exists. We group into the family as herd, and like animals that form larger communities we form into villages, towns, cities, provinces and nations. And is not the humble anthill more like the nations of mankind than it is different; it is no stretch to make such a comparison. It has a difference though, in that it is a nation of cooperative individual drones that cannot resist the impulse to live for the common needs of their underworld empire.

For every anthill of one million ants there is a spider's web or hutch that is occupied by one lone spider. The spider, individual in character, is not however acting outside of its instinct to be alone and thus cannot be regarded individualist; it does not eat other spiders, or try to trade other spiders the flies it catches so they can build a larger, more opulent web. The spider is an introvert. Individualism and exploitation are inexorably linked, and only the human has the ability to develop the drive to take advantage of their fellow animal.

Individualism does not exist as a precursor to itself, and it does not seem to develop solely by itself. It needs its own justification and validation otherwise it would be no more than a perverse desire to be regarded in the same vein as gluttony and greed. Vanity is the justification of individualism.

It is from a person's vainglorious desire that they justify a rapacious and avaricious behavior, and do not regard their behavior as anything but positive, as it is positive to their selves. The validation for individualism is luxury, or that is to say exclusive luxury, unnecessary luxury, and vulgar luxury. These luxuries go beyond the need for comfort and the aesthetic of form and function that should prevail in fair and sensible arrangements. Without vanity there is no luxury, and there can be comfort and obtuse comfort without reaching luxury.

When one is hungry they seek enough sustenance to feed themselves, and if they have a family that depends on them they seek enough sustenance to feed their family unit. Taste is the secondary consideration to adequate volume, and volume is second only to price or difficulty of procurement.

If the hungry decide to visit a restaurant it is the same animus that allows them to decide where to eat. Why then would one chose to pay far more to eat at a restaurant that has a menu in a foreign language, waiters that refuse to be polite, and portions that are likely to be smaller and made from unpronounceable articles?

This unmistakable trend is the vanity of choosing luxury. It is the vanity of one who can afford more, and pays for it rather than question if it is actually worth more. They are paying for the exclusivity, and the right to say that they can transgress where others cannot.

This may seem benign on the surface, as the rich man steps over the street beggar to walk to his four star restaurant. Has he not earned his treat? My point of course is that the rich man enjoys his splendor, but why does the splendor exist so far beyond what can typically be imagined.

Another example: if the typical cost of an automobile cost twenty-thousand dollars, why would a person pay two-hundred thousand? The answer as in the latter example can only be exclusivity. There is not much more comfort, and the automobile is a simple tool; I cannot perceive that a wealthy person would pay ten times the cost of the average hammer to instead have a golden plated hammer with a mink fur handle, but I have certainty that one is being produced somewhere.

To arrive at the ends of such luxuries is a vain endeavor. There is no luxury that comes cheap and there is no person without wealth who is unaware of this as a fact. Therefore the drive to obtain an unnecessary material as a sort of necessity is the drive to enrich oneself with the means to obtain the material.

The material is the vain robe in which one seeks to wrap themselves. Thus at great distress to one's current comforts they put an abundant amount of effort, or existing wealth, or criminality forth to obtain what little they desire. The only realization, or perception, derived from this is that they have yet to obtain enough, and greed sets in. More things and larger things, and greater exclusivity become their raison d'être as other exigencies are put aside.

 To satisfy their vain desire for luxury many persons have to be sacrificed. There is no wealth earned that does not profit from either low wage labor, gluttonous consumerism, or the sort of outright exploitation that cannot be euphemized - sweatshops and child labor are not without their justifiers. When wealth is achieved miserliness sets in, and the last chance for the individualist to return to society is bypassed.

They can return by way of redistributing their wealth in increased wages for their labor, the real charity of supporting others in their endeavors; or in the least paying a higher share to the state as taxes, so that the state can take on the philanthropic role that they have abandoned. Beyond this the individualist projects their mode of being so that others seem to desire to emulate them, and not project anger at them for their abundance and the illegitimacy of its acquisition while many more have nothing.

Ostentatiousness is but one of many of the characteristics that relate itself to the individualist's validation, and as there are many characteristics, this one in particular is a driver of the individualist's existence. The vulgar display of wealth and success designed to impress is typical of the individualist. Even in the face of a lack of significant wealth, one can easily perceive the individualist in their created splendor.

We can and indeed do often feel good about our selves, and feel even more satisfied when we accomplish an achievement. Whether or not the accomplishment leaves the individualist with the feeling of superiority would need a different type of scrutiny; however, it does leave them with the desire to expand their ends. The ostentatious character is thus shown when, from these ends, they erect monuments to their personality in overabundant terms. The mansions, the expensive jewels, and the like, are the trinkets and trophies for which they have toiled and which they have no shame in displaying.

Individualism has to have areas of triumph. Otherwise it would not be able to survive, as it is opposed to the strands that bind societies together. There are laudable individualists, and one has to make sure to differentiate them from the true, anti-social individualist. These of course are not Amish men with a dispassion and detachment from material life, not Franciscan Friars, or any form of particularly stoic persons.

Indeed any of them can be found in either the indulgences of individualism or promoting their own individualist forms of society that run counter to convention, or even counter to reality. These pro social individualists are not unpopular, and to that extent they leave posterity with the affect of their legacy, and an abundance of pretenders to their thrones.

The greatest triumph of individualism, and one of the present day's greatest devices for exploitation, is modern capitalism. There is not a "which comes first" question to be posed, the progression seems quite clear. As nations liberalized, and the individual was freer to pursue their own desires, they were freer to pursue commerce.

As this pursuit of commerce came with the realization that there can be wealth greater than that of the rulers of society, capitalism expanded, and outmoded mercantilism. As private wealth grew so too did political demands, which were principally demands to assist in the spreading of that wealth, and protection of it from foreign interests. Individualism grew in this period of political demand where men could indulge their desires, and even their presumptions to power.

Once individualists realized the power of capital, they assumed the mode of capitalist, and exploited material wealth, manpower, and territory, for every last gain. The capitalist-individualist was allowed to exploit for further centuries until the demands for limits to their power, and greater welfare became a fundamental part of the social contract.

It was now no longer enough to keep a nation safe from invasion, but a nation to must keep a people safe from cold and hunger and extortion or risk its own legitimacy. The individualist of course resisted this because it meant for the first time in their era of dominance that they were vulnerable to prevailing sentiment, and the state itself became no less than a rival.

The only way for a force to be resisted is for its counter force to exist and for the individualist the counter force is the humanist. We have seen these men and women in history in a variety of settings and posing various demands.

The constitution of the United States of America is in essence an individualist proclamation, built on the foundations of humanism. When Jesus Christ preached a new religion to the people, and offered himself as god on earth, one cannot disambiguate individualism in him, and what an ostentatious claim this was. However, the intention of his preaching was the liberation of mankind from its present spiritual, if not literal, chains.

And when Martin Luther tacked his thesis to the church walls he was fundamentally altering the highly organized cohesion of the Catholic Church, to the individualist strains of reformed and protestant churches we see today; although his drive was to liberate people from the exactions and rules of their rigid Papal system.

When his near name sake marched in America, Martin Luther King did so with the personality of a man apart from a typical man. The individualist's charisma is necessary to rally a group of people. The latter Luther did not eschew the aggrandizement of public speeches and conspicuous marches. He assumed a position right in front for the world to see, rather than print modest pamphlets or petitions. Neither did Gandhi, Darwin, Marx, Mohamed, Lincoln or any other liberator bypass the grandiose stage for humble reproach of power to be; there were many in their movements who did. It is through the influence of individualist individuals, who can set an example and be recognized as a leader, that collectives can be mobilized to perform and sacrifice for the dependence of society.

The only negative impact any of these men left, completely beyond their control, was their imitators. Those men who would use a similar position, title, or even the person's name to pursue an agenda or exploit for gain. It seems as if it is enough to be a black preacher today in America to be regarded with the same reverence as Dr. King. And one can scarcely see a Republican politician run for public office without comparing themselves or their programs to Ronald Reagan, as if that is objectively positive or even objectively true. It is only objectively exploitative.

Imitators are fundamentally individualist. And they lead us to a new form of exploitation, the cult of personality, which arises from the realization that personality or charisma can be used to sell a program.

The interregnum between an individual and the individualist is duplicitously expressed, by the individualist, as liberation and the preferred mode of being. They indeed do not have the desire for others to share in what they have, only to make sure that none attack them.

If the individual perceives that not only can they have what the individualist has, and it indeed is desirable to have, then they will defend the individualist as if they were already in that person's shoes. Putting forth such a clever ruse doesn't necessarily allude to conspiratorial means.

Here are the processes, and they are not conspiracy. The individualist does not understand specifically their desire to limit their own numbers; therefore I do not attribute to them that which we call conspiratorial action. What they do understand is that most of society can not have the same level of material that they do.

The most concrete way for these individualists to assuage society is by means of achieving a cult of personality with followers hewing to their principles. They broadcast their manner of being, i.e. their personality, and thus create a following to their principles.

The less austere conditions of individualism shouldn't be confused with the more sinister implications of absolutism in the form of dictatorship. The cult of personality, as it is commonly understood, organizes itself around an individual whom through the use of propaganda and coercive measures creates an idealized, oft heroic, image of themselves. It is typically for there to be flattery and praise of the person in question.

In the case of the individualist we see an appeal to the common acquisitiveness of mankind, and the program of convincing is done solely on these terms. Propaganda is replaced with marketing, and coercion with subtle or less than subtle convincing.

The political dictatorship does not necessarily need the means of cult of personality when it holds the monopoly of violence and coercion. There have of course been political dictators who used the cult of personality, especially in socialist dictatorships. They are perhaps more needed, or more dictated, by leaders who are not military dictators, because they lack the conviction that their rule is solid and backed by the violence of national arms.

In the hands of the individualist the cult of personality is employed in the same manner as the civilian political dictator. They are aware that they do not have violence or coercion readily available as a means of attainment, thus what is necessary is a following, a cult, as their proxy.

You will not find today a politician or social activist in a democratic country make demands for greater support systems for the people, who is not met with the reproach that says their measures will hinder the freedom of the people. The people to be hindered, of course, are the people who exploit the lack of support.

Take, for example, private health insurance companies. They would not make profit or would make less of a profit, if there is public insurance. That form of insurance would likely be at far lower cost to an individual. A grander share of people would pay in, and state revenue would be applied to the program which would stabilize the low cost.

When the cult of personality is activated, it represents the demands of the individualist en mass. The individualist is few in numbers and needs a multitude to represent their desire as less then rapacious. The mass of followers or cult thence create what looks like an interest, and by interest I mean a public interest, and therefore a good thing for society. The cult can be organized by means of populist rhetoric, and the modern media can be exploited to spread this rhetoric. The rhetoric of the object of the cult of personality compares to populism in that it is vague, non or pseudo intellectual, egalitarian, anti-elite, and ascribes a notion of civic principles 'lost' in today's society. The main difference, however, in populist and cult of personality rhetoric, is that the former is transient and will self terminate as its demands are equally transient, or its motives are; in the latter there is an interest in maintaining the veil of ideology for as long as the individualist needs to exploit it.

Populism, again, like the cult rhetoric is not intended to reflect on a specific person. Unlike the cult of personality for the political dictator, the person in question is not or not as much as import as the ideology, although they are seeking its benefits. What we also see when the individualist uses the cult of personality, and uses an actual person, they use a person whom the current society does not have direct access, and thus can not be questioned only interpreted to give the modern conception of individualist rhetoric legitimacy, by comparing vague phrases, concepts, or speeches.

Take for instance religious movements, Jesus' and Mohammed's works and doctrines were written many years after they had died, and even today, many more years later, when the stories are interpreted, they are often adjusted to fit the present day. If, to take a biblical example, Jesus says, "the meek shall inherit the earth", the modern preacher can say this means to keep one's self humble as that is the preferable mode to be, or that wealthy people are most likely bad people. The interpretation can be made in many ways, and it might just mean that the majority of people in the world will be poor.

Simplicity in rhetoric is the key to exploiting the cult of personality as the base will more likely be credulous, innocent, and or naïve. They will likely be motivated, by a form of comparative thinking. What I mean by this is that they will listen to the rhetoric, the simplicity of it, and its quotable phrases, and apply that level of thinking to whatever life situation they presently enjoy or don't enjoy.

For instance, to say that lower taxes means that a person has more income, is a literal manner of thinking, however when a politician says lower taxes, they avoid specificity because they know the average person will respond favorably to paying less. What the politician fails to say is first when you pay less you receive less. There is a depleted ability to provide state services and secure guarantees, and though this is itself is a simple phrase, it should be part of the complex discourse. Secondly nations have complex tax codes, and lower taxes may actually mean that one segment, the wealthier or the corporate, will have lower tax rates and the middle income segment pays more to make up for the loss of revenue.

The confusion of the individual with individualism can lead to confusion in how to judge whether or not the individualist is positive, neutral, or negative. Of course the argument from the individualist itself would have to be closely vetted, as that is a person, quite obviously, consumed with their own self projection, and likely incapable of reflection in earnest.

A person's responsibility for making moral judgments and taking actions that comport with a morality are themselves affected by whether or not they are subject to any level of individualism. If a person's moral agency reacts by doing what is in their own self-interest, the egoist, then they still have yet to broach the line of the individualist.

It is human to eat first and share what is left over. It is individualist to eat and throw away what is left over. If one is altruistic, or philanthropic then they are exceptional; if one participates in society and pays tax then they are an individual. However if one refuses to participate and return nutrient to the soil for which they sow, then one is the individualist, and there can be no positive view of that.

Individualism is supposed to express the existential worth of the individual to the extent that it opposes external interference. What a noble sentiment. However this is not at all how individualism really exists. Ironic to its own name, it seeks to prevent greater unambiguous systems from preventing the individualist from taking advantage of the greater mass of individuals.

Individualism stands opposed to religion, state, family, socialization, any human made constraint against swinishness and apathy. It changes as time and conditions change and allow it more space and over a wider plain to operate. Individualism is spawned by a desire to aggrandize oneself beyond mere self interest, and the means by which that is done is exploitative.

The aggrandizement which is spawned by the individualist strain comes from a desire to possess, that desire to possess comes from coveting already existing possessions, and this is greed. As the desire to possess pushes the individual to a nearly obtuse desire to possess, they begin their transition from cohesive individual to individualist. Knowledge of the means of possession is what finally wrenches the individualist out of the individual and away from society. Once the individualist designs the means for which they will extract currency or material goods, they must design the manner in which to continually exploit this new relationship.

This may seem benign, is a restaurateur really running against the common good? The simple answer is no, but when is anything simple. Restaurateurs are profiteers and for them to make a profit, they must charge enough to pay their labor, purchase goods, support themselves as owners and pay their business costs.

Now comes the exploitation; the restaurateur charges twice the value of the previously mentioned cost, and creates for themselves surplus capital. They do not distribute the surplus to labor, or even hire more labor. The restaurant patron is none the wiser, as they gladly pay. They pay even though the same amount of money could feed them for more days if they simply purchased groceries, and prepared their own meals. Why have they not simply reached the latter conclusion?

The restaurateur has convinced them, in advertising and the like, that his food is tasteful, convenient, and or cheap. Marketing and advertisement are not only simple sales tools, they project a conflated self estimate to the possible consumer, one which is either wholly untrue, spurious, or intentionally misleading to say the least.

I do not mean to convey that individualism, though exploitative as it is, only manifests itself in the moneyed interests of business, only that business is a prevalent arena of exploitation. Enterprise can be the bastion of cohesive man. For instance, if a business makes a profit, and hires more employees, or opens more franchises, it contributes to the community for which they are extracting capital. In this case business supports society, although simultaneously exploiting it.

Cohesive man and individual man exist simultaneously in the same person whereas individualist man exists separate and to himself. Cohesive man, or more apropos society, has two prominent aspects. In one aspect is the knowledge and faculty to dispose of nature and its forces, and extract its resources to convert them into wealth for the satisfaction of needs. In the second aspect there is the knowledge and faculty to create regulations to adjust coexistence in the latter, and the distributions of wealth.

The individualist is a virtual antagonist of society. Although society is a universal object of man as a social animal the individualist does not feel the same need to sacrifice, to do that which makes a common life standard possible. Therefore society has to be defended from the individualist, which is where we see the secondary of its aspects, its regulations, positioned in the manner in which they are. They have to protect everything from the individualist's rapacious impulses.

Society is not simply coerced into its state of existence. If it were to live up to the full extent of socialization the individualist would face an existential threat; and the contrary could lead to a complete fracturing of the social structure. From this assumption the individualist takes on the role of reactionary and prepares to attack, or influence the individual in society, to renounce their cohesive instincts.

Society has to reckon that there are present within society those with such destructive and dangerous anti-social impulses and it has to be prepared to counter them. The individualist's insecurities can be transgressed to quiescence if one realizes that society is not paralyzed to individualist reproach. We can apply the same regulation to individualism that we apply to nature, however adjusted to fit human emotion; we can implore, appease, appeal, or even bribe them, thereby influencing them and removing a part of their power.

An ordering of relations should be possible that would remove individualist dissatisfaction, simultaneously preserving society, by establishing the instinct to be social, so humanity would devote them self to the second aspect, creating and enjoying wealth.

PART TWO
THE SELF AS SUCH

There must be an analysis of the nature of the individual to know why they are not the individualist. There is a nature that one person holds, the nature of self inclination, which we usually label selfishness. It confuses many into thinking of the individual as the individualist. Yet considering a person or a person's actions as selfish, and selfishness as fundamentally negative is an illusory notion.

There simply is a misunderstanding of selfishness in reasonable persons. The mental disorders of anti-social personality disorder more readily embody the characteristic ascribed to selfishness; or it is the veil over the nature of cupidity. This can only mean that selfishness is misunderstood as it is applied to relative behavior. The thinking person who has the ability to feel genuine remorse and contemplates their actions takes into account the effect. This can not be described as selfish, however self serving of an action they have taken. The self serving aspect of action is easily better attributable to egoism; also an oft misunderstood term, confused with egotism. Of course I do not mean to undermine the *superior* moral acting of an altruist. It is simply not unethical or immoral to act in one's own self interest.

Quite often a thoughtful person will be faced with a quandary that will pit what is best for oneself versus what is best for, at least, one other person. The resulting decision leaves the person to be considered as unselfish and branded with moral approbation or selfish and thus illaudable. While the characteristic of the decision can be classed as such, I find it quite weak to then attribute that quality to a person, even if that person frequently makes choices of one kind or the other. Selfishness is not acquisitiveness or miserliness.

The reasonable person takes the same consideration when choosing that they take when they are giving or exchanging. When making a decision on these intercourses the consideration is what they are relinquishing is of less value to them then what they are receiving. The typical saying is that there are no losers in a fair trade, and the typical understanding is that there are. The selfish label is applied to a person who makes a decision for their own good, and the result is a perceivable, unfair interchange, that does not however imply a malicious intent.

A person who seeks for themselves is of a normal mind. When employed we ask to be given the highest possible wage. The firm's revenues are not taken into account when a wage earner asks for higher wages. Common sense would drive a person, in the eye of inflation, to ask for more in keeping up with ever escalating prices.

A person making a decision can not compare the good of their firm to the good of their family or own consumption. Is this not selfish? Well

29

of course an action taken with the self as paramount is a selfish action and yet this is not a selfish person, nor is this a reproachable action. Furthermore, if this same person makes a decision with income as their sole prerogative, one could hardly think them in the same vein as a brigand or mercenary.

With the consideration of comfort, good health, lack of want, quality shelter, and all of the things that make life livable one can make thoughtful decisions. And with only the reasonable thought process can one make unambiguous decisions. The pragmatic, empirical decision is always the decision closest to an acceptable reality.

If what is actual or real is reasonable then it makes sense to take the pragmatic decision. Everyone is a pragmatic realist, in that they live a life devoid of obvious and voluntary delusion; and as we are all realistic we will always make the most realistic choice and the most realistic choice will always be in our own favor.

One cannot have a discourse on the self without touching on the ego. The ego is I and self is what the designation, I, refers to; therefore the ego is self and as such I will use them in a synonymous fashion. The ego I have in mind is the psychological ego, or the considering of one's own self relative to others. A distinction is made which more properly shows the self as ego, and that is the distinction of egoism and egotism.

These words are so close as to sound synonymous, yet they describe phenomena that are different. The egoist is the one who says that his or her moral imperative is to act in accordance with their own inclination, while the egotist has an obsession with self; such an obsession can not help but result in a kind of Schadenfreude (deriving joy by harming another), or an anti-social malformation.

The self of course is susceptible to either influence, one possesses a dualism of both, yet one does not embody both at the same time. Is this then sublimation of one for the other? I would say no, but one is only influenced by one or the other. The egoist can relate to another, their relation is simply filtered (through) thru their juxtaposition while the egotist has the position without the filter. Thus it is the confronting of "you are like me and not me", with "you are not me and we are thus different." Our first person perspective leaves us as these selfish egos as our inclination or interpretation is always rendered as from our own points of view of the external.

What the ego allows in the self is three differentiations in appraisal, those are understandings of the difference inherent in, inclination (directed toward the self), interest (benefit to the self), and vantage (the result of fulfilling self desire or other's desire).

Starting with self-inclination the ego considers stimulus and judgment based upon and how one should or is likely to react to external forces. Inclination is very basic; it is an egoistical force of will. That is a

judgment made on whether or not taking types of actions is likely or unlikely. In a sense asking one's self, "do I feel up to it". With inclination there is not a question of risk of loss or possibility of gain, more of an appeal to animus. "I do not feel like it", then one is not inclined to do so, or "I feel like it", then I am inclined to do so.

External stimulus has to be directed toward a self for inclination to be an impetus. If egotism enters the equation of self inclination then it becomes, near permanent, disinclination. At that point inclination would involve valuing the stimulus rather than a pure force of will. And the more one values the less one is moved by inclination and the more one is relying on interest. Inclination is more closely egoist, and since it originates from the self, it is going to result in the self's positive reference.

Self-interest put in this context is less simple and more than what egoism encompasses. It is an egotistical force of valuing. The question here is, "what do or can I gain", and before interest animus takes place one must answer the question, usually in this sense, "I gain nothing" and will be unlikely to act, "I gain something" and am likely to act or, "I give something" and will not act.

This impersonal calculus is what the self does to make interest -based decisions. And it is hardly as opaque as the instances offered; specifically speaking one frequently gives something to gain something else. The unlikely giving in self-interest is giving something with no gain of any type. That description too needs further clarification as gain or no gain, are of different values; the gain is subjectively determined by an individual and can be immaterial. Pleasure is relatively immaterial yet one will give to gain it, which is a universal.

The other condition of the ego is its appraisal of vantage. The nature of this being advantage and disadvantage. And as such, egoism and egotism can effect vantage considerations. These are common words and their meaning is exactly what they are in a dictionary.

Interest and inclination are contained within both as positive-advantage, and negative-disadvantage. Egoism comes into the animus when one decides whether or not something positively results in fulfilling of one's desired agency – fulfilling their or another's aims. Egotism by contrast is whether or not something positively results in fulfilling one's desire only.

All ego appraisals share the sole ability to consider only from the first person, the self perspective. That is all that is possible for the ego; it is internal, existing only within oneself, looking externally through the periscope of self. The ego mediates and interprets the world of external stimulus to the self.

An individual is not automatically a self. Imagine if instead of referring to *I* or *me* and variations of those two words, replacing them with *one*. The only thing that can be inferred when speaking of *one* is that a person is being referenced as a person distinct from a multitude of persons.

That *one* is replaced with *I* or *me* when the facticity of existence becomes evident to the *one*. It does so from sensory realization of body and mind to conscious. As this realization is reflected upon the

33

consciousness the phenomenon of merely existing inscribes the essence of meaningful existence, transcending simple existence; thus *one* now becomes the *I* or *me*.

I or *me* then comes into the nature of the individual but it still has yet to become the self, and in that sense it is a positional referential as *I* or *me* distinguishes between *I* or *me* and *not I* or *not me*. For the *I* or *me* to finally become the self it has to do so transphenomenaly – it surpasses the knowledge of appearance. That is to say that is has qualities of more than its body. But how does the *I* or *me* evaluate these intrinsic qualities or even that it has intrinsic qualities? It achieves this transcendence by being conscious of being conscious of the external world; meaning that *I* or *me* becomes self by knowing that there is *other*.

This reflection is further possible as *I* or *me* judges what it reflects upon; I am pleased by it, I am disgusted by it, and so on. The judgments allow it to say that if *I* or *me* were the extent of my existence – in this sense *I* or *me* and *other* would be transpositional, which means they are two equal entities replaceable with each other as they are in the same relative position – and that said *I* or *me* would possess that which is negative.

To avert this *I* or *me* insists on self, so that it can be judged on what makes it unique apart from *other* phenomena. The positional referential is now a simple convention of rhetorical reference to the self. And once we finally have self we have the mode of being which is prior to self esteem, self-sacrifice, self-discipline, self-satisfaction, self-analysis, etcetera ad infinitum.

We do not cease to evolve at self; we simply end our distinction at that point. There are however more gradations to consider briefly. We have the ego, the 'self as such', and of course the individualist.

We already know the obtuse self which the individualist is and the ego is the self's consideration of the self relative to others, that which explicitly resides within the world of the mind as a conceptualization. That is the psychological ego with which self appraisal is driven by the nature of being an individual self, which we can not otherwise do. In this anything we do is reducible to pursuing our own self interests, i.e. reciprocal relationships are formed out of necessity not emotional connections, self-sacrifice or giving is pleasure of satisfaction, and altruism is perpetuation of the family and by extension the species.

When we speak of a "self as such" we do have something new because we are speaking of a person in the manner of actually being in the world, beyond the mental consideration of conscious, and placed into reality. Once we come out of our heads it becomes experiential to perceive selves not sublimating their urge to pursue their natural self interest. One, on the surface, seems to put their own interest ahead of those of the collective; though this is not quite the case.

If one pushes their way to the front of a line they will be fed first, that is a selfish, self-inclined action, and this may offend decorum. If they have not actively taken food from another then they have yet to do anything harmful. Every man by natural desire will prize that which is good for him. How could he do otherwise?

This reality of self assertion of self runs contrary to the moral culture of altruism, sacrifice, sympathy, community, love, or to be more succinct, the greater good. I suppose it would be difficult to have a cohesive society if everyone tried to supplant each other in the line. Then it would not be a society, it would be the, "war of all against all".

Are we really speaking of selfishness as the cause of consternation? It is such a misused word, applied so liberally, allowing the real menace to remain unnamed. The word selfish can only express that which the word means; self, which we already understand as referring to a unique person, I, me, ego, and individual. Its suffix -ish when attached to a noun denotes "belonging to".
So we can understand the word as we understand its more malign contemporaries, self-inclination, and self-interest, or advantage. If we look more closely at this rhetorical bogeyman of *selfishness*, and at actions it is assigned as agency to and their perpetrators, I see the same culprit, cupidity.

It is that eager or excessive desire to possess something, greed, avarice, or the green-eyed monster being protected behind the walls of "selfish as cause". Moreover, you will find cupidity behind many pernicious incarnations, it is the form other vices morph out of, that desire to possess.

When one uses selfishness as a repost that is what they are trying to say in fewer words, "you are attempting to possess that which I, your accuser, perceive as more than what you deserve". And if that is not the sentiment then what other negative sentiment could one imply; for an action to do harm there must be one for whom the action harms. Then one may say it is selfish to withhold that which you can give to help another.

Once again another try that does not land; for that action we have another title, miserliness. And miserliness too is a form of greed; it is tight-fistedness, a desire to possess that which one has to abundance. You may too think I have caught myself in that definition because it contains belonging to a self, and I say not quite. The agency of miserliness is still a desire to possess, the nature of the object in this case, one's own possessions, is incidental.

Selfishness is, though with its own attached stigma, a far softer accusation than greed and thus is preferred. The cultural negativity, and ingrained discomfort with greed restrain the accuser from using it, and the accused will hardly accept it. Greed is central to the nature of exploitation.

The desire to exploit, itself, does not exist as a desire in and of itself; it is an extension of the desire to seize. One wants not only to possess but to acquire ever more, which implies at less cost, as that which is expended is itself a possession. How does an employer enjoy more capital one asks, and what is the answer, by producing more, and how do they increase their profit margin, by cutting cost, in other words paying lower wages, firing employees, and increasing prices; exploitation.

Selfishness is not the negative that greed implicitly is, it does not take from others. I do though hesitate to call it moral; I can only accept that it is amoral rather than immoral. What is moral is extending our survival, it is the only implicit imperative given by the natural world; life is for living. A life of simple self-interest though may be a less than easy one to live, and so our self-interest assumes the nature of mutual interest.

Before we get that far we have to escape the state of nature. That then begs the question: would we be able to escape a state of absolute freedom, which implies the greatest level of self indulgence derived from unfettered freedom, given that self-interest, selfishness, is our default mode? I say yes because I do not see the state of nature as one of freedom. I see nature's restraints from its capricious indifference to life.

When analyzing a self in the state of nature it becomes difficult because there are stages of life, and as we all know the age of a person bears on their capacity to both be an individual and relate to others. I believe my illustration functions more succinctly if we consider a mature person.

The family relation must then already be implied; so our example of a person in nature already understands group living, and considers their family members as extensions of their self. The person too understands parental (mostly maternal) sacrifice and thus has the concept of doing for others and asking for nothing in return. Our person is also embedded in the group because they have a role in the family, giving them the inclination to stay a part of the group.

Because they have lived closely with their family they will have at some point witnessed a family member being injured. From this they draw two conclusions: one is that there are perceivable distress signals that indicate discomfort, as well as the second, learning how to empathize with distress because they know how an injury can feel.

The family does not leave our example of a person in nature without negative realities, indeed there are two in particular, malice and envy. Both are inevitable as the child can, let's say, envy his father's greater strength, and simultaneously feel maligned by the father's position as head of the family.

With this original position of familial socialization the person sets out into the world of nature to forage for eatable plants. Though mature the person in nature is still a youth compared to their parents and in their campaign of gathering takes delight in the sights of other animals as youth does, distracting from the task.

As they return with a less than expected amount the parents are unpleased. The father brought a boar to the family, and the mother drinkable water. The parents, knowing that a family cannot be sustained with less then what they need to eat punish our example by withholding all food, even that which the example brought back.

This experience has occurred before, and unable to oppose the father due to his relative strength, leaves the family unit. Thus we see the first act of self interest. This, though, was a rash example as the person was not sure where the mother got the water, and is not strong enough to catch a boar, he does know how to find eatable berries. The person is aware however that berries alone do not sustain them so they have to find out how to get water. The only knowledge they have is that another was able to do it, so the recourse becomes either learn how without training, or find another who knows it. Once they find another person that can gather water they have to figure out how to get the water for their self. They cannot simply kill the other person or they would only have water for the day. What is resolved then is a gift of berries in exchange for water.

The only way for each to keep what they now prize they have to keep the other person close, thus forming a mutual compact for assistance; combining their strengths to indulge their desire to have what they could not obtain themselves. And what is given up; at this point the freedom to roam, but that was not an interest of either, so they still possess their self interest, they are simply asserted thru another person.

How then does this move them out of nature to society? Indeed they have satiated their self interest, and not only that they are in a unit smaller than their own family. In a state of nature the diversity of life experience would likely be less various so many berry pickers will search for water gatherers, and as there are many types of berries, nuts, and other foliage our groups of two will mingle with other groups of two, living ever closer to exchange what they have for what they want.

Out of sexual interest the males and females will at some point mix, and produce berry picking children. This cultural similarity of the berry pickers allows them to identify and trade with each other; they now have a cultural milieu, though not yet a society.

What the berry pickers, in their new milieu, have forgotten is their boar catching parents, who were individually more powerful yet not culturally cohesive. What the berry pickers remember is the taste of boar and knowing that none are strong enough to catch one. They are faced with a new decision; they can either bring boar catchers into their milieu, or try themselves. Remembering their mistreatment at the hands of the catchers the berry pickers decide to catch boars on their own. The first few set out, and are unsuccessful, another group sets out, and one picker is gored by the boar, killing the picker. Realizing their inability, another group goes out, not as individuals, but as a mutual responsibility unit, a team, which will divide the catch.

Finally, success happens as a group of pickers bring a boar in. Yet there is another problem, one picker wants more than the others, so he kills a picker to get more. The other pickers in the group, now seeing this one as a threat come together in another team to punish the killer. Because of this they decide to divide the boar evenly to avoid further trouble; they each fear the loss of their own life so they chose the alternative that keeps them alive. And as they return to

41

their homes one picker has a thought, "my father controlled my family because he was the strongest, yet in our team the strength of one person was not sufficient."

The other pickers, drawing from the same experience came to the same conclusion. Following this genesis we see more self-interest in a desire to get at least as much boar as the others rather than none, and the realization that one is stronger as many and therefore more likely to survive. The berry pickers, from that trial and error, then organized mutual hunting parties, in which other pickers picked, and water gatherers gathered. After a generation the parents, who withheld from the next generation, passed away leaving them now gathered together as cultural groups of hunting and gathering peoples.

Though it would take other cultural developments for the pickers to develop into proto-governmental systems of tribes, they had progressed from the natural family to the socialized culture group. The principal of mutual self interest lead to taking the first step towards forming a society. As was illustrated, those who do not have the power to take advantage of their interest, and escape desperation decide they will live better if they make common cause. They begin to mix with others, and we call the result society. Therefore self-interest is not against society, it is its catalyst to escape the state of nature.

Actions reveal the relation of man with his world, and those actions are indubitably taken with self-inclination, for is that not how man is by nature? Looking from within to without, can he do any thing other? Then what does one risk by this self-inclined, selfish, behavior?

Ultimately, nothing! The implication of *risk* is that one has put up some value that they have the chance of forfeiting. In this case no value, at least no equivalent value, is being wagered.

The countervailing forces here are preservation of self versus perception of self (external perception). Perception of self is, more accurately, perspectivism, which asserts that no way of seeing the world can be definitively true, while maintaining the escape of positing that not all perspectives are equally valid. One then can know something by context, yet if the context changes so too does that something.

That something, though remaining constant, has a new meaning. We do this to interpret actions, and with actions being so numerous as to defy simply charting their implicit affects, we instead rely on categorization of principles. Drawing from these categories we have our pre-determined perspective.

Let's take justice for an example; how can one construe an action as just or unjust? Does one conform to a manifest and are their actions measurable to the extent that they do harm directly to another? Furthermore if one does something that another sees as distasteful, while not contradicting the manifest then is their ugliness just? If one drives their car through a red stop light are they then an unjust person? What if no harm was done to another person and they simply drove on to their destination without incident; and yet what if they strike a pedestrian while speeding up to cross through a yellow light before it changes to red?

These open questions are for you to answer, and you will not answer in the same way as another and many others. "Divergent answers" are the essence of perspective; justice is not the same for all. It would stand then that self-inclined actions only reach perspective, filtered thru aspects on preconceived categories. In other words, they are made to fit.

It may seem contradictory of me to have put forth the negative case for individualism then to put forth the positive case for selfishness. That, of course, is only if you look at this from an apportioned perspective. Indeed we are not speaking of two appeals that have a same significance.

They are not the same as comparing their reductions, individual and self, which are relative synonyms. Individualism appeals to a base instinct of self aggrandizement, while selfishness appeals to the interests of the self in that which belongs to the self. Individualism possesses the naïve assumption that all is done thru one's self, and the need from others is for them to implicitly do for one's own gain. Whereas self interest does not work without recognizing mutuality because one has to make up for shortcomings or prevent exploitation by giving up the right to exploit. In a system of individualism the latter prevails, more as a rule. In other words the one who makes out the best exploits most.

Individualism moreover has to rely on conversion of individuals to prepare its support system. People naturally resist exploitation, and the most well suited persons to convince them that this exploitation is non negative are those in their same position, their fellow exploited.

Selfishness does not need to rely on such scurrilous tactics as it only seeks to sustain itself; it is its own support system. There is no need to convert an altruist to selfishness. Indeed it serves the self interest of someone to have the individuals live in that mode of *other* mindedness.

Though it is highly likely that an individualist is self inclined, it is not implicit that this is the case. Appearance is not substance and substance is not hidden by it. One may, for instance, see an ostentatiously dressed individual. That may be a philanthropist enmeshed in expensive suits or silks, and yet it may just be an individualist on parade. A selfish person is characterized by actions they take, and actions are not superfluous they are the result of substance, so obviously appearance does not presume to reveal selfishness.

Selfishness as self-inclination is a hypothetical imperative or in other words it is merely good because it makes sense to act in one's own interest; it is reasonable. It is the pragmatic realization like that of the Irish Airman of W.B. Yeats' most famous poem: "nor law, nor duty bade me fight, nor public man, nor cheering crowds, a lonely impulse of delight drove to this tumult in the clouds." That "lonely impulse" of an Irish subject of British domination was an ignoring of the external and responding to the internal, the ego. To put it another way, the Irish Airman took flight because he alone wanted to.

45

A hypothetical imperative, furthermore, applies only conditionally and the condition is the self's appraisal of the situation it is in. In a given circumstance one is compelled to react: I am hungry thus I am impelled to eat, I am thirsty thus I am impelled to drink, and there are many more examples. What we see is the reality of the self replacing its objectivity; the objectivity being that the self is one person apart from others, the reality is one person who is *not* another person and possesses intrinsic needs. Combining the reality paradigm with the hypothetical imperative: I am hungry thus I get food for myself to eat.

It is quite easy to say that selfishness exists, and then to define it. Then what one makes of that definition is left to the subjectivity of their rationalization or misinterpretation. To give just one dictionary definition of selfishness: it is concern with one's own interests. And I like that word "concern", it conveys exactly what those for whom selfishness only connotes a negative seem to overlook.
That "concern" implies the ability to value, not just saying dogmatically that all rivers should flow into my ocean, rather I need what I need to survive and live. It would then be unfair of me to assert that as absolute, for it would become my own dogma which ignores the negative impacts of to much self-consideration.

What is needed then is distinction, and gradations in selfishness. But I would have to prevent myself from such a line of thought. Once we allow such evaluations we allow greed to slip back in and soften itself as a level of selfishness.

We may make the mistake of calling altruism a kind of selfishness. It is not as these are too contradictory. It will always be most sensible to speak of actions on their own terms, and perhaps apply the relative adjective to enhance the serious nature of the incidence, if that is required. As any distinction then I only see selfish and unselfish (implicitly not selfish).

We already know what it means to be selfish, and to ground what it means to be unselfish, especially without confusing it with being altruistic, presents one with a moment of pause. How does one approach it? It cannot simply be a negation; the construction would be peculiar, perhaps lacking meaning and a contradiction of terms of subject and predicate.

To negate "concern with one's own interests", we could say, "dis-concern with one's own interests", but that would be a contradiction because if it is one's interest that implies that they have a concern. We could phrase it, "concern with one's own disinterest", not quite a contradiction, but that does not describe unselfishness; it would only imply a self-interest in things that were related to another, and do not affect one's self. We call those types of people nosey.

We could then try to construct it as, "dis-concern with one's own disinterests", and that would not work because if one is not concerned about something they will not act upon it, especially if it is beyond their interest. A few more negations could be modeled using, "not one" in the place of one and "other" in the place of own, yet the results are the same. I would have to reason then that unselfishness is not simply a negation of selfishness, that it is a thing in itself.

The definition I prefer then is: the promotion of someone else's interests. That someone else is the "unself-" so if we look at a breakdown as we did before we have "unself-", not the self or someone else, and '-ish', when attached to a noun this means belonging to. The definition then fits well.

How then, if we start from the position of looking from within to without, resulting in self-interest, and if unselfishness does not seem to derive from mutual self interest, do we get to unselfishness? We go back to the ego and to self-inclination.

It would be easy to say that self interest ends where one makes a decision counter to their desire. This however is not the case as it is the self still making such a decision. What changes is the primacy of self-interest, and such primacy is vetted in inclination. If one is inclined to do something it is in their primary self interest to take the action. If the action results in promoting another person's interests, then it is unselfish, though it is in one's self interest to take that action. The real contradiction to the action being not in self interest is when one is compelled to take it, rather than be inclined to do so.

PART THREE
BEYOND THE SELF

A decisive importance for our judgment of the self lies in the assessment of what is harmful to the greater mass of society. That which oppresses and depresses and that which reverses those affects. If that is not understood then history has lavished many an example of mass revolt against the society at present to establish a new social order. We have made it to a point where we have placed the individual at the head of this social order; though I often wonder if that is truly the case when for an individual to succeed another individual must be harmed.

Under the guise of competition, also engraved in the contemporary social order, there is no outward revulsion at allowing people to fall ever lower, especially if the trade off is securing our own position. And with humanity set up as self inclined these conditions do not come with utter shock. There should be shock none the less.

Our self inclination does not prevent us from creating a society imbued with equality, indeed it is within our self interest to do so. Without social justice one is lead to the conclusion that our existential society of the individual is hardly a new social order, as what is harmful today seems only to be a repetition of what was harmful yesterday.

We live in a time in which the wealth of man reaches heights not imagined in previous epochs; the poverty though does not seem to abate. The common dilemma of the have-nots does not seem to fade away. It is understandable that the oppressed people should develop an intense hostility towards a society, or society in general, whose existence they make possible by their labor, but in whose wealth they have too small a share.

What emerges from such friction is a class of haves who are singularly devoted to the have-nots, and we have come to call them the altruists. One wonders in the human condition of self inclination, and in an era of individual indulgence how they emerge at all. Taking the altruist's existence as a given though, there is the persistent phenomena of the poor have-nots that becomes ever more curious. The phenomenon can be transcribed in one conjunction which expresses the full sentiment of their condition, and that is dehumanization. It is the denial of their existence by the haves who feel no pang of immorality to inequality which is constantly expressed in the dilemma of the urban setting.

In our daily travels we bypass beggars who are likely unwashed, yet we are clean; they have no definite place to go, yet you have a home and employment. And somehow they make us go out of our way to avoid them. En route to our destination we are likely to spend a few dollars on, let's say, coffee, a newspaper, gas, or transit; yet handing them a few coins or more seems like a burden. We cannot escape such displays of this unbalanced society so what is our response - we blind ourselves to that person's intrinsic nature and its similarity to our own; we do not face their disparity.

Given the nature of the self as fundamentally selfish how then do we find the existence of altruism in the world? Certainly that nature of giving without return is explicitly contradictory to self interest and advantage. It also cannot simply be explained through mutual assistance, as giving lacks mutuality, there is nothing being gained. Self inclination also does not explain why altruism exists; it only allows one to decide to give, or not to give. Where then is the wellspring?

It lies within a transcendent nature of the self which is encountered by a person when they separate from the other persons in the world of experience.

This nature is that of transpositionalism; the other person is recognized as an equal entity to the extent that they could replace each other extrinsically, in the sense of, "a person" replacing "a person". So in the less then literal sense existence can take the place of other existence.

Once one recognize the inherent the quality of a transpositional self, they have unlocked another aspect of significance, and that is equality itself. In equality we can now refer to the nature of mutual assistance. The self recognizes when being mutual it has a risk in being unequal, to the self. Therefore, the self inclination gains at least that which others can have, which implicitly presumes that others will receive a share - an independent particular share that they receive from which the self has none of.

Equality, from that point, becomes moral because it supports the only real moral imperative, to live one's own life, in other words to survive.

Inequality then is inherently negative. It creates a group of person, whom, to support their own survival will have to threaten the survival of others. For those who do not have a share, have-nots, they are not privy to the understanding of the nature of mutuality. As non-mutuality has threatened their survival the have-nots are reduced to beggars, who are aware of the possibility of mutuality and test it from the extreme position; extreme because they know that they ask for a share while not allowing one to be taken.

The other extreme position is that of thieves; they are also aware of the possibility of mutuality. With their survival treated as less important they enact that as their form of mutuality; their equality is devaluing the other person's survival as to transposition their own. They take money, food, or other goods, that which they do not have.

Altruism then could be posited one of two ways which do not possess mutual exclusivity. First it is, support of self by supporting the other, and second it is a moral obligation as derived from the moral imperative. Put differently, "I give so that if I ever have a need someone else can be counted on to give to me"; and for the other case, "I give so that I can maintain the equal expectation that my life is of paramount value to me and I do not want it taken by another".

Furthermore, if there is a wonder as to why some go to the furthest extent and some give at the bare minimum, that can be ascribed to perspective. If one perceives a greater gap between inequality and equality they will do more to fill and the converse for the person who perceives a smaller gap. It is the same as art appreciation, some will pay millions to own the Starry Night of Van Gogh, and while others would say it is only worth the materials it was made with.

There is another aspect of the perspective on what to give, which refers back to the transpositional. That is, while one perceives the other as equal they do not mistake them for themselves and so they consider what is being withdrawn from the first person, their own, position to make sure that they are not damaging themselves by overextension.

If you take off too much time from work to volunteer at a shelter, or contribute too much money to a charitable collection, then you will lose that job and ability to support yourself, and effectually you pauperize yourself. If you become a have-not then you not only can no longer give, you are now in the position of begging; and at the same time you fail in the imperative of living life, as you have eschewed the support system of your own survival.

Transpositionalism assumes the nature of psychological egoism, though there is something in psychological egoism that is not reached by transpositionalism. The disconnect between the two is essence, or quality, to put it another way. Transpositionalism only assumes that because two entities have the same relative position they are equivalent.

So let us take position one "a person" and position two "a person", obviously either position could be occupied by the different entity, and the essence remains the same. However, if the entities assume a unique quality, and become, in position one "an airline pilot" and in position two "a two year old girl", exchanging the position of the entities becomes unreasonable. If position one is flying an airplane, and position two is attending a day care center, then we clearly see the inability for transpositioning, as the unique characteristics in the essential nature of the entities in the scenario prevent them from assuming the other's position.

A two year old girl is highly unlikely to be able to pilot as complex a mechanism as an airplane, and an airline pilot is an adult – flight certification has an age requirement so one can empirically say the pilot *is* an adult – therefore not describable as a two year old child.

In psychological egoism there is essence added to the other; it is who the other is relative to the self, i.e. mother, father, brother, sister, friend, foe, partner, relative, stranger, master, or supplicant. Also, like each other, they connote a valuing action of "I or me" and "not I or not me", and also like each other they play a role in altruistic consideration. In psychological egoism altruism is perpetuation of the family, and in adding transposition the species can take the place of the family. Thus we come to a new concept, with psychological egoism contained therein, and that is familial transpositionalism.

One is then left with the question, is altruism reducible to perpetuation of family and species by extension? Furthermore what exigency is revealed within that concept? To pursue this question I present four equivalent concepts: equality, humanity, godliness (benevolence), and family. These concepts express a similar sentiment, which is that another is no less than the same as me. We all intrinsically possess these superficially disparate concepts.

Equality we already know, and which we can shorten to 'all having a similar share'. Why though does humanity imply all having a similar share? It does no: humanity implies an empirical standard by which an entity can be described as human. Thus all humans are no less than the same quality; we intrinsically possess a similar share.

Godliness (benevolence) needs a further expounding. By saying godliness we are saying that one possess the essence of goodness. That is the goodness implicit in the positive nature of existing as opposed to the negative nature implicit in *non*-existence. God here is a synonym for the nature of being, hence its coupling with the parenthetical, benevolence – showing good will. And so, just to clarify, when I say godliness (benevolence) is the goodness belonging to the nature of being. So if one simply exists they are imbued with godliness (benevolence).

Finally, we look at family, and ask how this implies that another is no less then myself. Well, as a thing in itself it does not imply this idea it has a structural difference to the other three. This was not an attempt at a diversion as you will see. The family, typically the people we know well and our blood relatives, are a grouping of persons, and therefore possess the other three concepts.

Because we know these persons well we instinctively lavish the majority of our attention upon them. And as our self interest puts us in mutuality compacts, most of them will be with family members. The ones we can not extend to related family we extend to created family; we find a spouse, bring children into the home, draw close to platonic friends and so forth. Our instinct then is too martial our resources to share with that family. Altruism feeds upon this instinct as familial transposition comes in to place.

As all three concepts are contained within the family and as we can extend our family to non-relatives, we can perceive any person as being family. The intermingling of concepts leaves us with a common human family that possesses a positive nature. Concluding then, we can only say comparing altruism to perpetuation of family is synthetic. Mostly because it does not respond to anything, it simply results from something, as an affect.

If altruism exists within a person, seemingly in spite of their self inclination then it seems plausible to say that a person is obligated to give. Indeed, that would seem to fall well within their self interest. Yet charity, and by extension altruism, are taken to mean freely chosen acts of kindness that reflect a generous inclination.

Such acts can be free from the desperate needs of people though givers are acutely aware that the need exists. Can we be obligated to act and at the same time free not to then? Of course we can, one simply has to understand the consequence of such nihilism though, and be prepared to counteract them or embrace them as an eventual reality.

With an obligation there are no less than the minimum extent to which they can be fulfilled, and the minimum extent of giving is paying taxes. There is a reason that one can pay less in taxes in the United States for giving money to not-for-profit organizations. Taxes are the support of the political society; conversely the political society is the support system of the individual.
Therefore, when the individual contributes to the society outside of the tax structure his or her social obligation is understood to be less than otherwise. The continual cycle of political society supporting individuals and individuals contributing to political society maintain the implicit and incontrovertible obligation to give.

For one to go beyond this giving, which is really give and take, they would have to impart the notion of obligation onto free giving, i.e.

charity. That cannot be done externally, so for one to impart they would have to understand the relationship as being implied intrinsically, and all will not which is why the altruist stands out amongst others. But what do they really understand, or misunderstand?

They understand that their fellow haves are not inclined, as they are, towards free giving. They understand that there are more have-nots than haves, relatively speaking. Finally, they understand that because of this disproportion there will be fewer contributing to the political society which means the political society will struggle to give a share to the have-nots.

As the have-nots are part of the society it is implied that they are due a share. So how does the political society make up for this, it defers to the individuals, who can only comprehend making up for this inequality by another form of un-equalizing, they pay a higher share into the system of taxes, seeking equilibrium. The altruist then gives another share; one that they were not compelled to give, to continue to decrease the disparity. Yet the unequal nature persists.

What is missed, especially by the altruist, the free giver, is the fundamental nature of the have-not, and that is they were promised the same share as the haves, yet the share they receive is different and less. The wrong thing is being given; the wrong need has been addressed. What the have-nots need is that which supports their self, in other words remedies that lead to self sufficiency.

It is the old cliché about teaching a man to fish; if you set a poor man up with work he can support himself. That is beyond recognizing a superficial need but imbuing that person with the dignity to sufficiently live their life. The altruist nearly misses this, but misses it enough as to see it as an end rather than a means. This misunderstanding leaves open a principal criticism.

Altruism is not impervious to critique. Indeed there is a prominent one; that altruism concedes power to the powerful haves and forces the poor have-nots into positions of supplication. The general problem is that of maintaining people in dependence, at the level of subsistence, and shut out from self sustainable material support. The malady surpasses its remedy, evolving or mutating like a cancer, as further generations are inducted into the regime of beggary. A pain killer, more of a placebo, is given to these people so they do not feel the full pain of barely living.

The civil codes and customs, the placebos, are put forth with lethargy of foresight for would be benefits. The result is a preference for and belief in sugar pills rather than a demand for preventing the disease from occurring and spreading.

Altruism plays a role in keeping the poor in order. Especially the doctrine that says it is okay to be a have-not, have-nots are the righteous ones, or your reward lies beyond life.

The meek shall inherit the earth; yet what sort of virtue entreats meekness. None, they will have nothing, because that is there nature, to let life pass them by, meekly. They shall inherit only that which they already possess and that is nothing. The biblical Jesus may not have even said such a convoluted thing as propounding the supremacy of complacency.

To what right, and in what way, could they assert a claim to the earth, as the meek? This has to then be, if it was ever even said, a clever misinterpretation; the meek cannot by their nature overthrow governments and take power, for if they did that they could hardly be described as meek. No, he would have to have been making a commentary, an observation that the number of have-nots will outnumber the haves, anywhere, and in any society. It will be the majority condition.

To then transition "majority condition" into the nature of being virtuous is basically creating an assumed principle by abstractly constructing, rationalizing, an idea with reason extracted from mean existence. To advocate a position as if it had been constructed it from an empirical, disinterested, experiment; yet what is really advocated is a moralization of what the have-nots already are, therefore to be moral is to stay low.

What could serve whom then to tell the masses to remain poor? This perhaps may not be the proper question, but the affect remains constant in these terms, "do not be mad at the haves for not leaving an equal share for the have-nots". The altruist can then say we will take the place of the haves, so take from us, and as the have-nots cannot return a share for lack of material, they only have their self to give. And what is the worth of a self to the other, the same as a child to a parent.

This leaves the altruist with another reproach, that of paternalism. Is altruism paternalism though, or is that an affect of the common measures taken in the name of charity? It can be both paternalistic in effect and affect, and this can be intentional or unintentional. If one takes care of another then they play the same role that a parent does to a child. What is to be avoided is allowing that care to be so overriding as to make the other so dependant that they cannot support themselves otherwise.

The best means for one to be helped is to be given a manner in which to reach the quantum of the means of singular existence, i.e. the minimum wage. That earning is requisite in the lowest, yet self capable, mode of life; its amount is appropriate for the maintenance of life. To find this for a person goes beyond charity to social stabilization, though not far enough to call it any form of equality.

Without this form of stabilization the path to real equality would be non-existent; although it is not itself equal. Economic stability is an indispensable condition of real equality. Whereas free giving is turning real equality into a sterile fiction that again tells the have-nots to be satisfied for you now have something. The offset here is that of charitably offering the have-nots certainty; and in the world of the altruist it is offering the have-not the certainty of a given standard. In other words, you can have what we have to give. That is opposed to the limited certainty in demanding an equal share from the haves.

It would be more beneficial if the poor have-nots could rally themselves to demand their quid pro quo, but it would be naïve of human nature to think that when one bares gifts that there will be none to receive them. The instances of people being ruined by freehanded largess are not too numerous. These are expenses were people are not likely to ruin themselves.

This is the role the haves play; as the possessors of enough capital as to be able to support as many people as they can, when the greater part of their wealth is a surplus to their own consumption. And this does harm, it prevents people from searching for their own solutions, as they think they have found one. Then the question becomes, to the have-nots, what to do to maintain the seemingly free gifts?

The only answer for them is deference to their benefactor, thus the establishment of the paternal relationship. Paternalism is a deprivation of liberty.

PART FOUR

THE WORLD OF THE MIND

We commonly come upon our self as a physical object in the world apart from other detached physical objects. To add intrinsic value we have to develop our nature of being unique more deeply within the world of our mind. The concept of the individual only implies the quantification of a singular unit, and the "I" a singular unit in a position designated as different from another single unit. Self, however, implies that there are distinguishing qualities that prevent an individual from being transpositioned with a different individual. The self is hardly confused with I; we, for example, introduce our self as, "I am myself", with *myself* replaced with our own name. Though we are not actually our own names, our names are the near unique quality that we maintain to distinguish who we are from who we are not.

To further develop this concept, we must venture into the world of the mind. That is the mind of abstract conceptualization and perspective, not of neurobiology, i.e. the brain. It is not simply something physical or something mechanically functional.

Within the world of the mind there is thought, followed by what we can label understanding and which further means understanding that a thought has occurred. This of course is followed by the use of that understanding, by abstracting it – summarizing it and attributing quality to it – in a concept. The procession continues to expression. This is where the totality of the thought, described by the prior process, emerges as what it will be beyond the mind, in other words in the world of reality. As the self is an expression it behooves one to understand the position of thought itself as being self causing, or if not least self causing then it needs to be understood that it is not an individual who stands as cause of thought.

The self may be extracted from the world of the mind but the relationship between mind and self presents a more curious relationship. Abstract concepts lay in the mind which is the result of thought; the self is one of those concepts. So where then do we get the concept "I think" that is to say if thinking is prior to "I" then how could we get to "I think"? Would it be too difficult to just say that after a thought occurs I interpret or I understand it! I suppose it might be.

Thinking has come to be conceived as active, and for there to be an activity there must be an agency – a cause – so we relax into the comfortable rhetorical combination of "I think". When we say "I" here we are making a further reference to the sense organ in which the as understood activity occurs. If that is the case then that sense organ, our mind is subject to the nature which the other sense organs, eyes, ears, nose, mouth, skin, and so forth, are subject to. Sense organs cannot be causes.

In other words, you see sights when using your eyes rather than you cause sights to occur by using your eyes. The sight already existed. In your mind you realize that you have had a thought. If we use an example; you are in a room with no entertainment, which means your mind is undistracted, and you are undistracted from the phenomena that it spawns. Suddenly a rhythmic sound occurs in your head, and from that you hear music. How could you have thought of the sound without being stimulated to do so? Or in other words, how could you not only have created such a complex thought as attributing a repetitive sound, to the nature of being rhythmic, and the culmination of that to the nature of being music, out of nothingness.

Is it not more likely that because you have at some point experienced what you consider music, that in the void of entertainment or otherwise distraction, that which was already in the mind was extrapolated as entertaining music! Perhaps in the same way that one understands darkness, because they have experienced light, and is in a position of being without light.

There are assertions that have to be made for there to be an "I think". First of course is that I am the one who thinks, and this is innocuous enough. It would be meaningless to try to refute the notion that my thoughts occur from or within me. Second, there must be a something that thinks. Here is where things begin to become murky, does the mind thinking, or the self, "I"? Third, thinking is an action, and by extension an effect of a being which is the cause, because for any action something must cause it to happen. Fourth, there is an "I", or an "I" prior to thought itself. Finally, "I think", asserts that I know what thinking is, and obviously I would know that without ever having thought of it, like an intuition.

With these assertions we can assess what has occurred as thinking and not feeling, i.e. reacting to something. However, if we are judging what occurred as thinking and not feeling, then that would imply the "I" indeed is not part of the process, but an interpreter of the event.

It would be prudent, if we cannot discern from the faculties of thinking and understanding, and mistake understanding as "I think", that we should look at where thinking begins. If we can at least agree that the mind is a sense organ, and I see no reason why we cannot come to agreement on those terms, than we can come to a common beginning as the primary cause of thought.

A sensory organ senses experience and acts as the mediator of such, e.g. the nose smells, the eye sees, and so on. So what then is the experience for the mind? That would be the world of experience. And before you say that, that is no different than saying the mind thinks by thinking, a means by a means, than you must come to the understanding in different terms.

By world of experience I mean anything that we say that we have experienced – i.e. sensed – from the physical to the sublime in the world. The eye sees color, the mind sees red. From that sense we begin to have a thought of, say, a traffic light being red. And from that understanding we extrapolate further what is in the world, for example the traffic signal is red, red traffic signals are equivalent to the command to stop my vehicle. Therefore, I need to stop my vehicle before I go beyond this traffic signal. An experience happened in the world, a thought occurred, one understood the thought, and interpreted it to draw out a broader concept.

In so much as a thought exists independent of one's ability to synthesize it, what one does with a thought beyond understanding it is what leads to such concepts as the self. The manner of willing those concepts into being belongs to the ability of one to do abstract conceptualization. Like solving a puzzle, one takes the disparate pieces to create a whole, except this puzzle does not have a universal result. That lack of universality is apparent in what results in an expression, and that is diversity. For instance, Japan and Nippon are different words and expressions. Nippon means nothing to the common English speaker, and Japan means nothing to the common Nihongo speaker; however, Nippon is Japan in Japanese, or Japan is Nippon in Nihongo (Japanese language). There meanings are equivocal but not equivalent, as they represent the same symbol, but do not typically mean the same thing to any individual person.

Essentially speaking, abstract conceptualization is creating "that out of this" or subjective from objective. In the prior example that would be *that* Japanese comes *out of this* Nihongo, as Nihongo already existed, as an object, to the speaker of that language, Japanese is a derivation from Nihongo to express it in English, subject to being spoken by an English speaker.

The thought being objective means that it can be nothing than that, a thought. Then the subjective is whatever is done with the thought; that is to say how it is abstracted for understanding and expression. Furthermore the object is perceived by the self as "this" and the abstraction as "that" – that which is or that which exists. The "this" simply describes the first person perspective by which our perception exists; a phenomenon occurs to me as this, and I see it as that. The thought belongs to the person in whose mind in which it occurred. In "that which is" there is the descriptive realization of that thought, or the expression of the thought in real terms, such as a word or image.

The two terms "that and this" can be juxtaposed to each other in rhetorical terms. They relate the self to its distance from an object; i.e. that as a term is used for further away objects and this as a term is used for nearer ones.

Words may be interchangeable, concepts are not so much. To think of the abstract conceptualization differently, we can term it as symbolism. Perhaps even better, symbol interpretation, in a structure of descending terms with thought itself as the apex, or symbol. The next level being input and output, followed by semantics and syntax, and then culminating at a base of representation as expression. The bricks of this pyramid of symbol interpretation represent a turn from what is – in the world of the mind – to what we present – in the world as such. A thought occurs and is thus input into the world of our mind, the output is our understanding of what that thought correlated to, we thus have a symbol.

Semantic applies a formulation to that symbol to represent it as its meaning; syntax arranges the symbol with corresponding symbols that allow it to then be expressed in the real world. The thought itself is independent of the expression. Two different expressions, as we saw earlier, correlate to the same symbol, however they are different from each other. Therefore, they are different in and of themselves. Things may occur in the same way within the mind; it is when they are expressed in the external world that they become unique.

PART FIVE
CONSIOUSNESS DEFINING THE SELF

When there is a person there is a self, an 'I'. This person is capable of thought, and contemplating existence. Therefore the phrase, "I think, therefore I am". This is the beginning of awareness and of personal philosophizing. If one can contemplate themselves, they can validate their existence as factual.

Even if all human life were revealed as a marionette show for a superior being, if the marionette is aware of itself it is an existing being with value. Awareness is reflective in this manner. It is conscious of itself being conscious and it thinks not only of what is in the physical world, but how it conceives its surroundings.

When one throws a ball, for instance, one does not become conscious that the ball has been thrown until after the ball leaves the hand; up to that point one was thinking of the throwing motion and contemplating its completion. Consciousness therefore is always aware of itself. One cannot exist as an individual, without being aware of themselves first, and secondly something outside of them self.

There are a billion people in China and another in India, and since I have not met a Chinese in person, I cannot say that any individual Chinese exists; nor can a Chinese say that I exist. We can only certify that our individual self exists and since there are persons outside of ourselves, and since I can look at a map and conclude that China exists can I then assume that Chinese people exist. In that sense reflective awareness is the fundamental nature of being.

Existing in space and time is not dependant on existence being defined externally. The intrinsic value of an individual is ascribed to themselves by themselves. Being and existing are devoid of a necessity to be defined. If they don't need to be defined then they have no need to be validated or acknowledged to say that they exist, they are not subjective. Existence is one of the minority conditions with facticity.

 Individual existence is life within a collective of persons with whom they have no relation; and to come together as a society something must occur. Estranged persons need more than mutual interests to band together, or remain separate. We can get to social cohesion by looking at what motivates the congeniality shared by absolute strangers, indifferent to one another's relative condition? Awareness can be the only way to explain. When one inquires how one is doing they do not actually care how that person's day is progressing, only that the person responds, and acknowledges the inquiry, typically with a trite and brief answer. It is more of an acknowledgment of one's self, or put differently a self that demands recognition to acknowledge its existence.

This is a type of mala fides pervasive in our common interaction. Mala fides, also known as bad faith, is an ingrained insincerity that more readily reflects the inward looking nature of human awareness. It would seem as if the awareness of mankind only exists as counterpoised to an opposite awareness.

There is something deeper than awareness and that is the self conscious. Consciousness is the self knowing itself and awareness is the self knowing everything that is not the self; and they are one in the same self, as inseparable parts.

There of course exists good faith, which is the deeper acknowledgement that I am a person, and recognize another as such, so I will greet them; we do not extend such courtesy to cats and dogs. Is such affirmative interaction, however, a necessary reaction if we exist freely to ourselves and self aware?

Mala fide duplicity is the nature of superficial interaction. It is considered double mindedness, saying one thing and meaning something else, meaning nothing at all, or having a contradictory thought. It may not be as sinister as an insult or intent to harm, but it is a false emotion, and therefore I regard it as negative. I do not care to validate or acknowledge another person's existence, in the same way that I do not care about them if they have not entered my presence and am completely unaware of them as a person.

If what I have put forth sounds harsh, then reality is harsh, for this is true of all people except the altruist. If a person does not regard their interactions as having permanence then the depth of interaction is typically equally shallow. This does not damage the person of whom the inquisition is made, because they have the same vain sentiment and desire for the interaction to terminate after validation.

For the person whom additional validation is required, what typically follows the dismissible greeting is the relatable anecdote. Once again, there is no depth, only a desire for a response. Any phrase regarding the state of the weather is an obvious example; two persons in the same space and time perceive the same meteorological event yet commentary is readily supplied to analyze the obvious, "it is raining hard...good thing I have an umbrella...yes me too".

The purpose of this exchange is to acknowledge that the self exists in that space and time and to validate that existence by the perception of another self. What is really being said is, I am in a heavy rain storm, and am happy that I have an umbrella. If one were to respond as not having an umbrella, the typical response would be feckless remorse, or the rare altruist in good faith, surrendering an umbrella to satisfy their need to help. I can rephrase my postulate as such, people do not, 'think therefore they are', they are if another thinks of them.

If a mala fide interaction does not take place then it would seem none are worse than they were prior. There may perhaps be offenses, but what is more or less authentic, offense or insincerity? The phenomenological nature of 'offense' is a highly personalized one, as it must make an appeal to the self's conscious.

In that offense exists, it is perceived differently by any different person. What divides the differences of person, ultimately divides the differentiation in conscious perception of the external stimulus that results to some as offense, while to others it is perceived as utterly benign.

The differences of person I class as such, sex and sexuality, race and nationality, social standing i.e. wealth and poverty, and religion; anything beyond these classifications I consider subsets of these already existing classes. How we perceive these differences, I do not feel of necessity to delve into, only to say that consciousness needs to perceive an "other", to perceive an own condition.

To put that in a different way, I am female because there is a something that I perceive as a male, and I am not that, and there are only two perceptible existences in sex, thus I am what is denominated female. Terming myself thus I am open to be offended by anything that devalues the nature of being female. The only thing in terms of offense that devalues the nature of an existence is that which does so rhetorically, an insult.

Devaluating the nature of existence in personhood – the quality of being a person – is transmitted from the abstract to the rhetorical once it takes on the qualities of being written, illustrated or spoken. Conscious perception must then assume the relation of the rhetoric as ambiguous and benign or unambiguous and thus negative.

The lack of ambiguity comes from direct reference to a class; for example, the statement, "women are weak". This is an un-interpretable statement and the object therefore is being held as less than the other objects of its classification. The corresponding response is what we then call offense.

What further drives the response is that the rhetoric is a lampoon from the "other" in the class, in this instance man. However if the statement is ambiguous, "a woman may have difficulty lifting that heavy box", the offense derived would have to be subjective, because the statement would need to be interpolated to be the equivalent of the prior statement. Beyond this the offense will be difficult to consciously perceive by the other, as they do not possess the qualities of the offended party, and cannot realistically sympathize with, not only the perception, but the literal impact of the offense. The greatest that the other can do is empathize.

For further instance, the literal impact of man regarding women as weaker is man denying women employment in physically laborious enterprise or the military policy that prevents women from serving in combat roles. The individual is free to make their choices, and the most freeing choice is the choice to simply exist. To exist as they see most fit.

If one avoids duplicitous interaction then one avoids the inevitable falseness of false consolation and false friendship. How disappointing must it must be to truly feel that you need someone and they not be there, yet how lonely it must feel to feel friendless.

Consciousness is always, consciousness *of* something, and thus must be actively used to conceive anything outside of itself as confirmation of reality. When one conceives an 'other' outside of themselves, they need a depth of emotional reaction that can be ascribed to the feeling of sympathy. To truly sympathize with another there must be a shared emotion-experience for conscious reference.

Without this shared emotion-experience any attempt to draw near to another person's experience is more like empathy. This empathizing seeks to take another person's lived experience and relate them to and assimilate to the self, to make the self conscious the center of action, and thus that which actually exists.

This relative experience is, once again, a mala fide interaction of one conscious with another. I cannot sympathize with a person who has a flat tire if I have never owned a car; so I search for a similar story, perhaps one where I am stranded. My attempt to relate my experience is more of an attempt to usurp the emotional moment, and re-appropriate it for my own purpose of asking that others sympathize with the situation as mine. The context of this discourse can be as such, "I had a flat the other day, and it made me late for work...I know how you feel, I was stranded at the bus stop last week and had to walk home".

As you can see it is an attempt of the conscious to recreate the situation for itself to validate its own existence. The respondent could have stopped at the word feel, or said, "I cannot imagine how you feel", and asked a probing question, such as, "was the tire difficult to replace". This would have required the conscious to acknowledge that another exists, not a large stretch for consciousness to do.

Consciousness can exist in good faith. The *something* that consciousness is aware of is indeed an opposite consciousness, and not solely for the purpose of acknowledgement also for the purpose of acknowledging. This nature of consciousness is equivalent to the emotional state of amorism but with more equanimity. We find in this good faith consciousness participatory awareness, which is an opening of consciousness to intimate participation.

For consciousness to participate it first comes to the awareness of something as not being itself, and therefore having its own consciousness. With this realization it seeks interactive validation...greeting another person. When the two persons are familiars the conscious furthers the participation and an inquisition is proffered...inquiring how another person's day has been.

The interaction does not take on the bona fides character, without regard to their prior familiarity, until the post response...the day is described. The post response and the reflective conscious can either describe a similar day, mala fides, or inquire further...that day sounds interesting, say more about this aspect of it. The consciousness draws as close to its counter consciousness as do two persons with loving feelings towards one another.

The equanimity in the interaction, of consciousness alone, is that it recognizes the other conscious as equally it's opposite, thus it's reasoning for interaction in the first place. We do not see this same equality with lovers, as their awareness of each other, leads to an awareness of dominant and subdued characteristics. Or a male recognizes a female, vice versa, and for a homosexual person, the nature of interaction is for something opposite in another person's characteristics of the same sex.

Bona fides must respond with the consideration of the other consciousness as paramount. It does however have the seemingly mala fides affect of validating itself, as the sympathetic listener; the difference is that the concern is the other not the self.

As sympathy is to mala fides, empathy is to bona fides. To be empathetic means to assume the effects of circumstances as relative to one's own self. To sympathize is to attempt to assume the emotional feeling, or the deeper feeling, of the affects of circumstances, as both relative to one's self and in the context relative to the original person. These two words are often confused with one another; however, empathy is sympathy sans emotion.

To feel how another feels, to sympathize, the consciousness has to reconstruct the emotion, and respond with an un-equivalent emotion, a similar emotion at a less intense emotional level. If a consciousness is able to sympathize at the same level or greater, for example, one person losses a loved one yet a friend sobs more or even as much, then it is more likely due to a defect, not in the consciousness but in the deeper mind of the friend. We empathize because we generally care about the object of our awareness.

Do I exist as an actual self, is it thru my self's deeper indulgence in its self or the reflective conscious of the self. After the self's first task, of realizing that it is conscious, is complete it undertakes its second task, realizing that there are things external to the self, this is where it has to decide what constitutes an extension of the actual self, or a separate conscious.

Every instance in which the self conscious perceives another conscious is sees it's identical and other, similar to a mirror reflection, and from there has to say that this is me yet not me in spite of its likeness to me. It is similar. Therefore, we cannot have a sense of being a self without the contribution of another self. Self consciousness can recognize itself within itself, and before or without recognizing the other. However, when confronted with this transposition, it has to decide what must be its reaction.

The self has two options, to negate the other self and or to assimilate the other self. It thus becomes inherent in consciousness to either negate, and make the self the only self, thus contracting within the self, otherwise referred to as introversion; or in consciousness to assimilate and add other selves to the conscious, thus expanding beyond the self, otherwise referred to as extroversion.

As consciousness expands and contracts it then has to deal with its next level of anxiety. First for the negating self, it has to have a notion of self that says I am the only thing that exists. This is a negative self, and the thorough going solipsist, extremely preoccupied with indulging its own ego. This is also the self that simply exists, as it lacks the desire to integrate it lacks the ability to change. Now for the assimilating self, ever expanding, it faces an enduring identity problem, and has a need to return to itself to assume its authenticity.

Consciousness assimilates and expands thru the motivation to exist for itself, by adding to and aggrandizing itself. The consciousness, though existing for its self, exists as mediated from other consciousness. Therefore, it has a freedom to think about itself and be thought about by others.

With consciousness encountering another self consciousness it finds it not so easy to return to its self and becomes uncertain with other consciousness. This uncertainty leads the assimilating and expanding conscious to negate and contract, to protect its selfness, because what it fears is that it will be assimilated its self. Self conscious wants to be certain of its self, and so far as it has been assimilating and negating parallel consciousness it is ultimately trying to establish a type of certainty of itself, because it is indeed primarily its own actual self.

To answer the initial question then, to exist as an actual self, a conscious must encounter other consciousness; it can then decide whether or not to engage with other consciousness. And if there is a need to encounter than engagement becomes highly and frequently likely.

If one does not want to engage then there is recourse. The self conscious can perceive its identical, reflective consciousness, as its equally identical self, and thus an extension of itself in the manner of it being a tool and thus an object. To therefore objectify the other self is to say that another person is only important to me for whatever material exigency, of my own and not theirs, which they fulfill.

Everything that the conscious perceives as other than itself is liable to not simply be perceived as the conscious' equal and opposite but rather an extension of itself. And when the conscious concludes something as extending its self beyond itself it is contemplating a thing as being an object. This objectification is not the mere acknowledgement that something has the quality of existing; no it has to exist for the reason of self indulgence.

For something to exist as an object it merely has to exist. However, for the self to consider it in the mode of objectifying it the object must play a role to the self, thus being rendered a tool for the self. A hammer, for instance, is considered a thing that is not the self. It is taken up by the self, to complete the task of driving a nail into a piece of wood. The self could not do this with its own hand, or foot, or forehead, not with any of its bodily extremities, so it adds to its hand a metal hammer. The self then undertakes an action, hammering.

An action is something only a self can take, and not an object. Indeed, an object only takes action by the will of the self, because it does not itself possess a willful faculty. Once the action has ceased the object has not ceased to be an object; but what can the self do with an object that it has made a part of itself, and yet not attached to its body? If the object has not been made part of the other self than for the extending over it the object becomes a property to the self.

Turning an object into property completes its objectification, as the self says that this thing is now only definable as a part of the self, i.e. this is *my* hammer. A thing that can be objectified can always be added to the self, it furthermore is an object, and it does not however mean that it cannot be the other self.

The objectification of the other self involves multiple aspects. First, the self has to recognize a parallel conscious, to some extent, in another self to be objectified. Parallel conscious in this instance is only parallel in that the self is considering a consciousness that is the other, yet not an equal. Since it is simply other, the self may now, in the manner of the selves being reflections of selves, consider this other as an extension of its self. With this as the consideration one is free to think of the other as being only as important to their self as what that other does strictly for one's own self. Or in other words, one does not need to speak to a door man, only enter or exit as the door man opens the door.

Objectification of the other self does not simply end at utility, because as with the hammer one has to do something with the object as a new extent of the self. There is a caveat in the case of the other self, though, it has its own awareness and will attempt to interact; you may not greet the doorman but the doorman is sure to greet you. For the self in this case it has to turn to negation.

If the self assimilates then it says the other is an equal self and not an object. To negate in this sense, one could ignore the doorman's greeting and give him the cold shoulder, and not find out who *he* is. The doorman, therefore, is my doorman, who only exists, within my world, to open and close the door for me.

The self is a reflective being; consciousness and awareness are equally reflective. They have to find their other and relate that to themselves in order to perceive anything other than the self. The perpetual interactions of consciousness are apparent and recursive in their inescapability.

One may choose to disengage with other selves, thus negating them or engage thus assimilating them. In assimilating we see the more readily prevalent reaction. And assimilating has a negative tendency, as we assimilate our equal and opposite self becomes more like our self and our self becomes more like our equal opposite.

A reflection in consciousness does not function differently than a mirror reflection, it is what we perceive our self to be; and as when we look in a mirror and adjust something ill fitting rather than adjusting the mirror, we make the adjustment to our self, and do so to make our self in the reflection more appealing. How can consciousness, though typically shared on the social level of personal interactions reach the point of so many persons being affected similarly by so many experiences? The relative similarities that strike the scope of human consciousness would, to me, suggest that there is more than reflective conscious, which assimilates all of human society.

It is hard to pin down exactly what creates integrated reflective conscious because as we see so much human similarity we see human divergence. Divergence, however, does not suggest a full un-integration as anyone could look at the larger aspects of a society and attribute many divergences on environmental exigencies.

The integrated reflective conscious functions like the associated press, in that as the AP receives a story it disseminates it to other media outlets, and from those outlets the story is picked up by even more outlets. The integrated reflective conscious, which I refer to as the "big conscious", takes in experience from any society, disseminates it to other societies and the more peripheral societies then pick it up, and the process reverberates in the opposite direction.

And once again environmental factors determine what a society assimilates from any experience. We see the literalness of big conscious's effect where we see shared human expressions; otherwise exemplified as, a kiss being a show of affection in all nations, all peoples have a language, or a language like English is spoken on three not physically connected continents from America to Australia. All people have music, aesthetic appreciation, dietary injunctions, and the list continues. Mankind is invariably similar, though it has yet to fully assimilate itself, as we prefer to amplify what is different, thus we have societies negating other societies and returning to their own selfness. As self inclined as a society may be the expansive reach of big conscious cannot be fully negated. With a more integrated world we see cultural norms giving way to general expectations, i.e. democratic government or free market economics; sameness comes with the enjoinment of benefits.

The big conscious of the world and the big conscious of a society are similar yet different. A society has a self contained big conscious that is the product of its collection of selves and reflected from society back to the self as social customs, mores, and ethics. The self of an individual is even less escapable to the assimilating nature of societal big conscious, because they will share the same environment. Therefore, environmental exigency will not be available to explain any divergence.

We see societal big conscious in things such as religion, the difference of languages per society and as a subset the differences of accent, the liberalness or conservatism in a society, the philosophy of a society, and many other concepts that make it distinguishable as its own society.

Not all societies have been widely integrated with the big conscious. Many tribes have been found in the Amazons that have yet to contact the wider world, and their customs have not affected nor been affected by it. Can a society, which has already integrated then decouple from the big conscious? The answer would have to be a resounding yes, and an equal no.

Society self has characteristics of the other as part of itself. It then has as its device of decoupling from big conscious, negation. Once a society begins to negate, and return to what it considers its authentic self, it goes thru the pains associated with contraction. Also, to the other self societies this contracting society will seem highly inauthentic, as it defies the nature which it assimilated to establish. In-authentic societies are, furthermore, rife for calamity; as a society struggles to redefine its selfness it seeks to remove the otherness within its self, and otherness is never removed peacefully.

It seems to be recurrent in history that societies will negate or try to negate big conscious, and since this cannot be done peacefully, can a society purposefully not integrate. The answer this time is only no. Since society is not a monolith, an experience may have a general affect. A segment may be affected differently or not at all. An experience, say, may result in super natural belief yet some will remain agnostic and unbelieving; there is no religious community that does not have atheists among them. Therefore, one must conclude that a society is enslaved to circumstance, and thus must integrate and negate. Even a society at the greatest heights of isolation will at some point be subjected to experience external to its self.

Divergence based on environmental exigency is not purposeful non-integration. Since this is not intentional, it does not show that a society does not want, and is not aware of the assimilating forces of big conscious, to integrate, only that it cannot.

The subconscious is not readily accessible thru normal introspection; it is expressed as the result of a multifarious cause. With the subconscious as the vast store of suppressed and unused awareness it is to the self what is prior to any other experience external to the self conscious. An experience external to the self conscious is anything outside of the self and is not the self.

Subconscious itself is external to the self and separated from the conscious, extending beyond its abilities in the same way that the world around us extends beyond our vision, even if this does not seem to be the case. Within the subconscious we contain all of our experience in the notion of a form and access the form thru recollections, either autonomous recollections or aforethought recollections.

The notion of form is acknowledging that when we think of anything we have to have something in mind, when we speak of something, write something, draw, paint, any means of expression we have a notion of what it means simply by thinking of it at all. We verify the same concepts meaning, from the subconscious, by using the conscious; when you draw a line you literally create the minds image of a line. The form that comes from autonomous recollection is the one that makes up the majority of recall from the subconscious; it is opening a door instead of walking into it, or looking at a chair before you sit on it, to make sure there is a chair below you. Autonomous recollection just occurs, and in this case results in the conscious acts of opening and looking.

Aforethought recollection on the other hand is, put simply, a conscious attempt to access the subconscious. For this reflection to occur there needs to be a cause to consider. We do not have all of our knowledge readily available, waiting in a holster for the draw.

To conceive of aforethought reflection, consider yourself thinking of any abstract concept. While you are thinking other like assumptions, and contingencies arise, and they were not apparent before. And they do not become apparent without the cause, for you would not conceive of a thing or react to an event if the thing or event did not cause you too.

All of self conscious is the concordant result of subconscious and awareness. To catch a fish you need a body of water and a fishing pole. The vastness of the water with its multitude of fish flow in their own direction as the pole and line and lure reach in to grab the desired object, the fish.

When one sets out, earnestly, to catch fish they will catch, in the least, a fish. Their problem is that all they can guarantee is that they can lower their line into water, what comes out and in what quantity and quality is not guaranteed. Introspection cannot pull from the subconscious. If we had that access to all that we have taken in this would be a world of incredible genius.

Aforethought is the attempt at introspection in the subconscious, and the result will be a something; however, it will not be all of what we have as experience, knowledge and understanding. If our fisherman sets out to catch a salmon and hooks a sardine, he has less of a fish but it is a fish none the less. In this manner, subconscious continually contains all of our experience. When they say that you never forget how to ride a bike, this is where, 'how to ride a bike', is swimming around.

And though we may never forget, we do not climb on the seat with the same ability as when we learn. But why do some ride better, and some catch bass, when that is what they set out for. For their purpose they have moved a piece of their subconscious to the forefront of conscious with long extended reflection; they draw often upon the subconscious for redundant material. The fisherman, who fishes in the same lake daily for hours, and knowing what type of fish lives there, should expect to catch multiple fish of that kind.

The subconscious plays a role in the interactions between conscious persons being mala fide or bona fide interactions. The mala fide interaction, the shallow interaction, is equally shallow in its reflection or autonomous in reflection. Greeting someone, with a hello or hand wave, or head nod, and nothing more, is as much a reflex as blinking or breathing. Whereas greeting someone with a hug and or a hand shake, as a show of familiarity, implies a deeper awareness of that second person, and a use of aforethought to engage that person with shared reflections, or memories.

With good and bad faith in our self, as deep as our subconscious we would do better to judge that which makes an authentic personal experience. We authenticate our material possessions to make certain that they will fulfill our material exigencies. We do not seem to do the same with a parallel consciousness; we simply accept its otherness without interrogative.

One can and readily does perceive when another is communicating with them in a manner that is insincere and would prefer the lack of actualized interaction to no interaction at all. It is as if a slight interjection is as much of a validating remark as an honest exchange of information. Beyond that one cannot encounter a parallel consciousness without being pressured to interact with it. When the self does interact, and even with a simple interjection, it has to sacrifice its own characteristics as one's personality conforms to the norms of what are generally considered standard greetings.

One seems to be most authentic when one tries to fulfill material needs or build relationships that will last; our conscious self is thus seeking its own perpetuation. What the self needs for its own perpetuation is diffuse. However, its actions have to leave it as being definable and distinguishable as its own self and not a contingency of an assimilated self.

When the self becomes fully assimilated it does not, however, become something contrary to authentic, or in-authentic, it simply ceases to exist. It becomes the proverbial face in the crowd, and the crowd, as a whole, assumes the nature of the existing self; one person, obviously, cannot constitute a crowd. For a self to be fully in-authentic it has to first establish a nature, for it to then exist in-authentically it has to contradict its own nature. If the nature of the self is to allow itself to be assimilated to a greater self, once it attempts to negate that greater self, it is then acting in-authentically; and it will be in-authentic until it either returns to itself and establishes that as its nature, or re-assimilates into the greater self.

It is typically difficult to perceive authenticity in another person and when we have interactions that are bona fide we are clearly recognizing another self as a self; therefore in this instance it will be even more difficult to perceive authenticity rather than it being the case that any bona fide interaction is authentic.

For a bona fide interaction or relationship to exist a minimum of four conditions must exist between two selves: There must be participatory awareness with the conscious open to intimate participation, interactive validation with response and engagement, sharing of and gathering of more than superfluous information, and finally the two conscious's must acknowledge the other as its equal opposite or parallel in awareness.

The nature of consciousness, that it expands and or contracts, is what leads a bona fide interaction to be in-authentic. A negation may not typically occur from a bona fide interaction because when one self is contracting, the assimilating self will try to consume it, forcing a reciprocal response of consciousness expansion.

From the attempt to assimilate too we see one self doing that which it will not typically do; offering information to gain information, offering false information to create a response, giving spurious information, and acknowledging another self as equal and opposite simply to relate to the other self, rather than objectify it. We, therefore, see a falsification of the key aspects of a bona fide interaction. This is therefore an in-authentic interaction, as it is contrary to the nature of this type of interaction. This, in a sense, is the essence of lying to, misleading, and manipulation a person.

Where a bona fide interaction can be in-authentic a mala fide one is always in-authentic; this may seem like a contradiction, for it is the nature of mala fides to be in-authentic, so an authentic mala fide interaction is being in-authentic. Yes that is the case mala fides is a perpetuated contradiction. It only, though, confirms that when you interact in bad faith the interaction has the nature of being in-authentic; it is a positive lie or a real falsification. That which characterizes mala fides is its indifference toward otherness from an inward looking perspective, its detached superficiality, and its obtuse self validation. Expanding and contracting are not what drives mala fides to be inauthentic; it is that way by its very nature, being in bad faith.

Self awareness can be viewed as being the overall structure which includes all of consciousness, subconscious, experience, and awareness as layers. First the self as conscious, second the subconscious, third experience, and fourth awareness, each relying on the interaction of its fellow contingent parts. Where, though, does this layering begin, end, and revolve?

Knowing the beginning is to know the nature of the layers of self awareness. The beginning and inner most layer of self awareness is the self. The self is considered dually with the conscious, or the self knowing that it is an entity that exists. As the self knows that it is first an entity it knows second that there are entities that are not its self, external entities.

External entities are accumulated by the self in its vast store of information the subconscious. You forget experience once a form of this information emerges from the subconscious to into the perceivable conscious it is translated as awareness. These of course are not mutually exclusive, contingent parts as all, without regard to the sub conscious, are relatively useless without their other relatives.

A comatose person is unconscious, unaware, and unresponsive to external stimuli. However, their subconscious still functions; if it did not they would awaken as a complete tabula rasa. Some do awake less functional but they retain knowledge of things which means their subconscious is persistently functioning.

It is often difficult to deduce where the original cause is for self awareness and it may seem that experience preempts all else. Experience is any occurrence tied that stimulates an abstract perception in our basic senses and needs no other confirmation; a smell, sight, sound, taste, or touch sensation. Therefore, we ask if experience informs awareness, thus informing consciousness and ultimately added to subconscious.

If this is the case then when an apple falls from a tree and lands on the ground while one is watching, how does consciousness translate this occurrence? If experience comes first than the act of falling must be completed before one can be aware of it, and then be conscious of it as it has happened. In this sense one cannot be aware of something as it is in the process of occurring, nor can they anticipate that the process might indeed take place.

If the person sees the apple detach from the tree limb, and turns around with the apple in mid freefall, and does not hear the apple hit the ground, then they have not experienced the event. For the person to conclude the fate of the apple they would have to return to their position, but the apple is already on the ground. Their experience now is that of the apple being on the ground, and a hole is left in their awareness; how did the apple, which detached from the branch, come to be upon the ground. Experience is therefore limited as it cannot carry an incomplete action to the level of self consciousness.

For something to fully be brought to self conscious it must then begin prior to experience. The subconscious then is a layer of self awareness that will precede experience. It is in the mind and therefore exists before an external experience can affect self awareness. One accesses their subconscious thru reflective processes of recollection. And we qualify the recollection via the same basic sense with which we qualify experience.

An experience may not be the first cause of self awareness, but it is the information agent for the subconscious. Experience adds to subconscious information that it can recall for comparative intuition. Once the subconscious connects the missing strands of experience we have a resulting awareness. Consequently, we realize our apple has detached from the tree, fallen, and landed on the ground, not because we experience it but because the subconscious can connect the experiences, especially the one we missed, falling.

Though the subconscious and external experience may seem interchangeable, they are not. Because the subconscious is in the mind, and the mind is always inside of one's self, subconscious too will be inside of the self. And as our self is always first and consciousness, is the realization of our self as a self, that leaves the placing of awareness. As the self exists, and subconscious collects external experiences, awareness is the collective and revolving result.

Awareness is the self's acknowledgement that external experience is something, first other than the self and second something in and of its self. This acknowledgement is the outermost layer, and yet is immediately turned inward for validation of the self being aware. If the self does not acknowledge a thing but experiences it, then that thing stops at awareness. I may, for example, be aware of another nation outside of my own, however if I never see a map of it I am aware and not self aware; the nature of this place avoids my conscious and is stored in my subconscious for future recollections.

Experience, though contained within our self awareness, is everything in the world, and the self is one thing within the world. Before there is even a self there is experience, and if there were no self the locus of experience would abide. The self does not need experience to be a self either, or at least it does not need experience to consider its self a self. When experience is being interpreted it is being filtered thru sensory perception. The core senses that one typically has of taste, touch, smell, sight, and sound are all that can reach the self, from experience.

Once the self has experienced an occurrence, and that occurrence has been perceived by sensory intake, than the self is aware of an experience and may be able to conceive of it materially. This material awareness is the last awareness one can have before trying to form a logical concept; occurrence has now progressed to being in the mind as an intuition, or otherwise as an assumption. An assumption then leads to the process of reasoning, which can either be a rationalization or knowing.

Experience a-priori is better known to us as nature, or to some as the Supreme Being. This is pure experience, or the occurrence which exists prior to the self's perception, and with no need of the self to verify it. The occurrence simply happens, and it may be misinterpreted from the point in which it reaches our senses, our awareness, our reason, rationalization, and our knowledge. That does not detract from its being.

Experience a-priori does not involve the self. The self being created is itself an experience for other selves, and not for the self; everyone has been born, yet none have experienced being born, in that they could not interpret the event as it happened.

Occurrences are added to a forming self, and the self is unable to use them until it develops its subconscious; the new born child can be given the experience of being shown a book, but without the faculty to reflect on the this sight as having bookness – the essence of being a book - the experience is meaningless to the child. An occurrence to our senses is simply a thing "becoming" to the self and does not yet possess the quality of being a thing in and of its self. Experience a-priori, furthermore, cannot its self be a self because oneself is not capable of recognizing it because it has not yet reached one's self, and it is not capable of recognizing anything.

Sound is prior to being heard which leads to, for example, hearing music; odor is prior to being inhaled which leads to smelling pungent; tart is prior to being licked which leads to tasting sour; texture is prior to being touched which leads to feeling rough; and color is prior to being seen which leads to seeing red. What this all amounts to is occurrences being filtered by senses, which translate those occurrences into abstract perceptions.

The perception is unique to the self, and in that sense a perception is always correct. It is correct in that when one self sees a red ball and the same ball is seen by a second self as orange, neither self can falsify the other with mere perception; because a self can only have its own abstract perception. I cannot look thru another person's eyes nor can they mine. Perception is abstract because it can only conceive of an incomplete and, as in the prior example, differently perceivable occurrence. Sound can reach one's self that perceives it as music and another that perceives a noise.

Experience a-posteriori is what the self ends up with after perceiving an occurrence. A sound occurs – experience a-priori, the self hears the sound and perceives music – abstract perception, and the self affirms to itself that it is indeed hearing the sound of music – experience a-posteriori. The sound of music, in this example, assumes the quality of being material, and it is now a thing. It is still not correct though. To generalize the thing as being music is to make an assumption. At this stage it is more like a thing with the qualities that can be compared to music; to the self it is music and if the self wants others to have that concept, it must engage a process of reasoning.

PART SIX

HOW ONE LOOKS AT THE WORLD

What is the importance of being earnest to a person? Indeed, are we being honest when we tell the truth to another or are we using honest deceptions to tell a version of *a* truth? I have no intent to impress upon you dubious contradictions, rather to avail you of a skeptical perspective.

Do not offer me *truth,* instead give me elucidation, and I will decide on its value. And if you will have truth, then at least know what you have. Where mankind is reconciled in is pursuit of truth, only an absolutist can claim impartiality regarding what most view as incomplete.

The indolence inspired by possessors of truth is actively detrimental to deeper understanding and progress in all arenas. It would be simple and to some preferable if truth simply existed, and established by some immutable law, external to mankind, rather than be arrived at with much error in the process, thru the struggle of existence.

Only thru the search for truth can we see a depth in life, and an ugliness which underlies existence. Utopia was not be the island of perfection and thus inhabited by those who know the truth as such. It did not exist; it was not a place where one could aspire to end up. If one had that wish it would have to be created, and to create it one would have to capitulate to really existing conditions that would not be wholly ideal to all thus making paradise a non paradise, truth a non-truth.

Beyond that, there is nothing that we can lay bare hands on and I describe as firm, and you describe as malleable, without describing the same space and time only in different terms. There is that which I can label as untrue; I cannot say that there is truth still, only that which is complex or inexplicable. Truth is a desire; it is within the abstract reality in which we live. And the only reality is the nature of life which is life and then death, creation and deconstruction, existence and non-existence.

There is often the demand to introduce complexity to situations where what is simple is more likely the better answer. That is the essence of Ockham's razor, that the simplest of explanations is the most preferable; however no person really applies this level of parsimony to anything in life.

We seem to live with the modern, incorrect translation of the razor that says the simplest explanation is most likely the correct one. I have to say, frankly, that if life were so simple it would be unbearable. Living this way is almost akin to reducing human decisiveness to the more pragmatic exigencies of wild animals. The simplest of theories, too, are hardly the ones we see as the vindicators of a thing. What is science without complexity?

A person, however, does not need to completely examine every aspect of every detail of an event, or entity to understand it. This would be an anal retentive and (vain) vein endeavor. These indeed were not William of Ockham's intentions, to make us all simpletons; indeed, the quote in most of its versions is, "Plurality must never be posited without necessity." That is hardly the same as keeping it simple. There are not pluralities of ways to examine, for instance, a sporting event. Yet there exist a plethora of sports media. The sports media is functionally simplifying what is already simple, i.e. to win a sports game you need to outscore your opponent. The rest is simply superstructure to the layman.

The sports consumer however purveys the complexity of strategy and nuance, and the other sports theory: is your task to score more points than your opponent or to prevent your opponent from scoring more points than yourself. This may sound like the ambiguous existential quandary that it is, but delving into this consideration is largely important. It determines how you set your strategy and or which players you choose for your team.

Intentional simplifications exist because to some they are simply more comfortable than thinking and for others a more complex thought is meaningless to them. I understand that there are multiple, unique, equally complex, and character saturated dialects that make up the whole of the Chinese language, and I am content to accept that truth in those terms. I have no interest in learning Chinese, or conjecturing in that tongue. For the American linguist, the diplomat to China or Malaysia or Singapore, of course the contrary is the case, and the difference between Cantonese and the Beijing dialect are oceanic gulfs to be traversed. Complexity is circumspect and it is life.

Another instance is the shape of the planet; there was a time when we were on a flat disk, at the center of the universe. The contrary is now the accepted case, as we have pictures of the earth from the outside, and circumnavigation as proofs of the spherical shape, and heliocentrism and gravity to show the earth's position vis-à-vis the sun. Since we cannot all travel beyond the stratosphere to look down, or comprehend astrophysics, we are satisfied with accepting the proofs, acquired from intensive processes, as true. Yet as we have not acquired personal conviction from experience we can be persuaded otherwise by equally intense explanations.

The proper shape in which a truth exists can only be the system that describes it. A truth may be delivered in many ways and by many more persons, but what they are delivering comes primarily from one of four different ways: there is subjective truth, objective truth, mathematical truth, and scientific truth. And to not cause confusion these terms can be further disambiguated.

The subjective truth is the truth that belongs to the personal conception of the truth, or the thinking subject, rather than the object being considered, or in other words "it is true to me because".

Objective is not quite the opposite of subjective, though its truth belongs to the nature of the object and not the affects from the object.

Furthermore, it is not influence by personal emotions as those lead to interpretations or prejudices, and it can therefore be described as a lifeless universal. Mathematical truth may seem to be a form of objective truth, but it is not quite, its principle concern is correctness in counting, its conclusions can though be described as universal, read objective.

An objective truth can be incorrect yet universally accepted, where as a mathematical truth has to be correct, as verified by its formula if it cannot be than it is incorrect, and thus untrue. Then there is scientific truth which involves forming and testing hypotheses that can be proven false by testing observed data. Once again this is a truth that can be called objective, but that again is not the case for the same reasons.

The first aspect of truth with which I will treat is that of the subjective, and to do so I must begin by asking you a question; if I said to you that my dog, who was standing still in front of me waiting for a treat that she can only receive when I give her the still command and she corresponds by standing still, was wagging her tail vigorously, then does she deserve the treat?

You may toss her the dog biscuit, assuming that she did what you asked. That she was standing still though, was not a proper statement of the case, for how could she be concurrently standing still and in motion; it would reason more to say that part of her was moving and part of her was still. This example is only a mere reflection on subjective truth but it does clearly illustrate what we do to accept a subjective state. By that I mean our minds have no other power of conception than that of thinking and forming adequate ideas. And the most adequate ideas are justified beliefs. One can believe a thing without it being born out with experienced evidence; however they will still need to justify that belief, at least, to themselves.

There is another way that truth can be subjective and that is that it can be a progressive unfolding truth; or in other terms a malleable truth, an incomplete truth, or simply, a current truth or opinion truth. I consider these four terms as mutually exclusive, contingent parts, of the whole that is progressive unfolding truth.

First, though, I would like to show a fully progressive unfolding truth: Is a rose forever a rose; the bud, which the plant is in the beginning, disappears in the emergence of the blossom, the former is thus negated by the latter, similarly when the blossom opens and we have now a rose, the blossom is negated as the false manifestation of the plant, and beyond this when the fruit of the plant then emerges – the rose hip – if you are growing the plant for the fruit then that negates its prior and the fruit is the truth of the plant, its true form.

Overall, a progressive unfolding truth is made from parts of a unity with mutual incompatibility and mutual necessity. These parts, as incompatible, supplant one another and yet because they are not

105

distinguishable as parts of a progression they are necessary to each other to form the whole.

From this then one can only get close to the truth, or to put it in another phrasing, you may purchase a rose bud, grow a rose, and pick a rose hip. All of these verb-predicate relations describe what is true at that stage of one object. They all have truth value. And from this example we can see how three contingencies fall comfortably into place; with the form of the plant being malleable because it grows from bud to flower to fruit. It is incomplete because describing the plant in any form does not describe its other forms, and finally current because one describes the plant only in the stage that it is in, and what they desire, flower or fruit. I could describe opinion truth in this example, but I fear it may be too vague and thus requires a stand-alone example.

The connotation of *opinion* in this case of opinion truth can be viewed in these terms; the Beatles are a great music group, I like their music, and they have sold millions of records. The former part of the statement is justified by the latter; however, the justification is only a self justification, that is to say they only inform a person of the nature of themselves.

What these justifications do, though, is make it more difficult to conceive the contrary. I actually do not like the Beatles, but because they have sold so many records and to many generations of people, I am compelled to see the justification of them as being great. It is a valid opinion. They have been made great by the superficial standard that they are subject to – recording sales.

There are two manners of logic that correspond to two manners of truth in particular, though not exclusively, and while we are on the topic of subjective truth it is pertinent to introduce its correlative manner of logic. Inductive logic is that manner which corresponds to subjective truth; the other is deductive logic which corresponds to objective truth. Induction is when one proceeds from evidence to what is most probable. For example, all newspapers I have seen are grey, therefore newspapers are gray. If I was asked by someone to describe a newspaper, my description would therefore include the grayness of it, and my description would therefore be true.

Newspapers though are not universally the same color, indeed USA Today is printed on white paper, and not gray – gray paper is newsprint. So my description, made with inductive logic, is subjectively true, because it incompletely described newspapers as they were subject to my conception. What would follow is, adjusting my description to, newspapers are typically gray, being true or not based on considering USA Today and the like as not being newspapers. I must also mention that a subjective truth is not a falsification or rationalization, because a falsification or rationalization can be proven not true or to have very low truth value.

It is a confusion of adjectives when we use the term objective in place of true so coming forth from the topic of subjective truth to objective truth, I will stay on the logic relation and you will see why they have their own connotations. The logic that correlates to objective truth is deductive logic, and this manner of logic is as such; the premise is self evident and therefore the conclusion is evident, and what you are doing is tracing a line of derivation. This is exemplified as such: I am related to my father, my father is related to his father, and therefore I am related to my father's father. This example may seem bland, but that is because an objective truth cannot do anything more than provide a lifeless universal as it is only the conclusion of the premise. One cannot, for instance have an objective opinion.

For something to be described in such a way would make it a contradiction, and if some part of a thing is not evident by another part than the entire conception cannot have enough truth value to be considered as true by an objective standard. Furthermore, objective truth is concerned with knowing *that* and not knowing *how*, and from that can only be a thing, and not an abstraction or metaphysical or a thing in itself.

In other words, that a wall is a wall can be objective, what a wall does though – hold up a building or divide a room – cannot because it does not say that which a wall is rather how it relates to other objects.

Owing to an objective truth's inability to describe a thing in itself it cannot describe an affect. This is primarily why it is termed objective, it stops at an object's being; the nature of the object and not what the object does in relation to other objects or does in space and time. An affect is a subjective truth, for example I hand you a baseball, and we both agree that the object is a ball, but you do not use it to play the game of Baseball, you use it to play fetch with your dog. What it is has not changed – objective – what it does has – subjective.

Affects will seem objective when they correspond to objective truths. However, when they are subjected to deeper scrutiny the affects show the malleability of a progressive unfolding truth, and are therefore subjective. I can ask thusly, does aspirin relive headaches? The postulate would not lead one to know what aspirin is, so since it asks what it does the object is the effect of taking an aspirin. An affirmative premise would then be, "yes if I take an aspirin…", and the affirmative conclusion would follow, "I can heal my headache".

If you answer yes then what you are describing to me is the affect of an affect and not the object of the effect of taking aspirin. Therefore, the conclusion is not evident from the premise, and would be the subject of the situation of taking an aspirin. If you use a negative premise, "no, aspirin…", and the corollary negative conclusion, "does not heal a headache", then this would be an untrue statement as it ignores the subjective truth.

The proper truth in this case is that aspirin inhibits cyclooxygenasis in the brain; which is what it indeed does. To get to aspirin curing a headache you must extrapolate on the affects of the effect; inhibited cyclooxygenasis decreases the production of lipid compounds and these compounds regulate the contraction and relaxation of smooth muscle tissue, i.e. the pressure that causes the headache. Therefore, the affect of that affect of the effect of taking aspirin is an alleviated headache.

The progressive affects relieved the headache not the aspirin. Furthermore, aspirin may have the progressive affect of relieving pain or preventing heart attacks, or of causing stomach bleeding, so its affects are true to the subject that it is used for. What is objectively true about an affect is only that there is an affect, or that an affect is an affect.

Objective truth can be incorrect; as long as a premise and conclusion concur something will be described as an object. Though this is the case objective will ultimately be equated with a mathematical truth. They both follow the same line of deduction, premise to conclusion, where the conclusion is correct because the premise is correct. If your premise is one added to one your conclusion is two. Math has the additional condition of the premise and conclusion being equivalent; therefore, one added to one equals two – the representation of the multitude of ones that is one and a different one grouped together. Because they are equivalent, it is a correct conclusion to say that they are.

Mathematical truth is a different type of truth because it is a self contained truth concerned with correctness, which is perhaps a better word than truth. Only understanding of how a mathematical formula works and the utility of it allows a person to understand whether or not a mathematic formula is correct. The concern of mathematical truth is correctness in accounting anything more than one or less than one. For something to be mathematically true it has to be provable by a mathematical formula and if it is incorrect by that formula it is untrue.

A mathematical truth is self contained by mathematicians, and a mathematician in this sense is anyone who knows how to use a mathematical formula. Therefore I could prove an addition true to most adults, they contain the knowledge, but I would not be able to prove the same to a child of young age and no education. To those same adults it would be unlikely that I could explain quantum mechanics, or prove something by it.

The inability of persons to understand the formula and utility would not detract from a correct conclusion, only the ability to proclaim the conclusion as universally true. A mathematician derives a proposition from a pattern, and then resolves that proposition by arguments which are sufficient enough to convince other mathematicians that they are true.

Logic is the result of proper reasoning, and mathematical truth is logical correctness. Reason is purely deductive, uncritical of its assumptions, and object driven. Most are familiar with the stale phrase, cold and calculating, well there is a reason that we have this conjunctive phrase. From this mathematicians can prove counting, measurement, and geospatial relationships. The base of mathematical truth and which forms its logical core is simple counting. For every value of one's is assigned a corresponding symbol, i.e. a two corresponds to a one and a different one grouped together, a three

'

corresponds to a one a different one and another different one grouped together, and so on into infinity.

The logical step up from the base is lower arithmetic; conclusions derived when using the traditional operations of addition, subtraction, multiplication and division. And then the final part, which allows a mathematician to deduce, is numbers that are less than one, i.e. fractions and decimals, zero, and negative numbers. With these cores a mathematician can build up to more complex systems and codify that which is correct, thus that which is mathematically true.

Scientific truth too has a relation to mathematical truth; as math has its formula as a method of proof science has its scientific method. They differ in that for a scientific consideration there has to be a hypothesis, and the conclusion is typically a theory and sometimes a law, thus not absolutely correct but provable.

The circumscription of a scientific truth lies in the method by which that truth is proven. And that method, the scientific method, belongs to understanding. The power of a mind is derived from understanding and to understand something is to understand its cause, *the why* and its effects.

The general scientific truths, its general laws, such as the law of gravity, describe the causes and effects as they are demonstrated by practice and application via the scientific method. From this working out an effect is explained by the essence of its cause and the more that a cause or number of causes – complex cause –

acquiesce together to arouse an effect, the greater the value of truth the effect or theory, will possess. That theory is then not harmful to a scientific truth.

The method for creating scientific truths is culminated by a ladder of techniques for investigating cause and effect, by gathering measurable evidence, and subjecting that evidence to specific principles. An experience or observance occurs, causing an inquisition and the scientific method follows this inquisition with a hypothesis – a conception, not to be confused with an inquisition that can be proven wrong – and then the systematic measurement and experiment, testing and formulation to a conclusion, and finally the modification of the hypothesis into a theory. The process extricates that which binds cause to affect the nature of a phenomenon. And the theory explains why the nature behaves in the way described in the conclusion. It answers the original question, and any questions created by hypothesizing and experimenting. The theory itself, though preceding a natural or general law, there to describes a scientific truth, as it has proven for understanding cause and effect.

The ultimate conclusion of the scientific method is more prominently a theory, before time and rigor confer on it the status of being a law, popular consumption regards the accepting of the theory as the acceptance of a subjective truth, while some elements regard it as having a low enough truth value to be untrue.

Those that label it a subjective truth too, are more likely inferring that it is an incomplete truth, either subject to the predilections of the scientist in question, or consider any part of their method as being wrongly implemented and thus bad science. Those regarding the theory as untrue are biased, whether or not there bias has a justification as bias rarely does, or beset by a viewpoint that has been contradicted by the theory.

We have two popular examples in the theory of evolution a theory of global warming, and to avoid myself being considered a partisan in either theory debate, I would urge the reader to investigate the opposing views to these theories, and the theories themselves, rather than elaborate on them. What is at odds with scientific truth is just that though, because it ends at theory the layman can simply dismiss it as untrue without having been acted upon by the method that concluded the theory. For something then to be a scientific truth we must not rely on the un-inquisitorial laymen and rather the method and the community of scientists, those learned persons of science. Therefore, a scientific truth is that which is provable by the scientific method as verified by a scientist.

How we learn a thing, that is how we understand the things we know, is the same as how we consider a truth. In all when we learn we subject points of view to general principles first, to work up to a general comprehension of a known concept. We then support and or refute what we understand. Then we use comparative classifications to apprehend our comprehension, as it relates to other understandings; and finally we can pass serious judgment upon it as a truth or falsity.

When the comprehension has been penetrated by serious speculative effort, the understanding of the things we know will retain its appropriate place as truth. Therefore, when we learn it is truth as *posse ad esse* (possible to actual) or from known to confirmed. Simply learning is not sufficient enough to possess a truth. To simply learn is to have knowledge unqualified, to stop at subjecting points of view to general principals. From that one would, in a turn a phrase, *know that* and not *know how*; or to be more exemplary, one would know what something is, i.e. I know a wrist watch tells time, and one would not know how something works, i.e. I don't know how a wrist watch tells time.

When we do learn a thing we obtain knowledge of particularity which is numbers to one another, they know addition. Learning is therefore an act in objectification, though learning does not simply lead to an objective truth. What we learn is the object of what we are thought. The object, most generally, is knowledge, which pre-exists to learning then exists in a new form after. What comes before is "knowing things" and these known things are better termed as justified beliefs. The belief is simply the thought that a thing exists in a form and the justification the grounds for the belief.

At this point knowledge is a belief condition. Once we subject this proto-knowledge to learning and arrive at a different knowledge, we have an understood condition. Knowledge now has its original condition and an enhancement, becoming what it should be, a justified understanding. When we can finally say 'I know' then we have a truth.

Therefore, truth is known knowledge, and yet knowledge is not always truth.

What knowledge is, is telling the truth to our self, it is our own personal truth, our perspective. And since one cannot live in isolation from other persons then our perspective is subject to any other perspective's influence and the other perspectives from our own. What we have then is the other notion of how we learn a thing and that is, or I should say those are mimicking or reflecting, relating, and translating or interpreting. To learn by mimicking we accept what we are taught due to the nature of the teacher. This is without bearing upon our understanding, and considered as being a true manner of justifying a conclusion and by extension the conclusion is true.

A child, for example, is taught math problems. The child may not understand why 2x2=4; however, they see that this method leads to that conclusion, so whenever they see 2x2 it will only be true to say it equals 4.

Mimicking is limited as when the variable 2 is changed the child may not be able to provide the correct answer. Where mimicking fails one has to relate to find their truth. When we use a relative perspective this must then be based on methodological understanding, i.e. when the underpinnings of multiplication become clear to the child, they can adjust when variables 2x2 becomes 3x2. The child can apply the multiplication concept because the variables have changed not the relative idea. For the child to apply their newly learned perspective to the world they have to then be able to translate its conceptual meaning so that the representative values of 2x2=4 is the same as their understanding of a situation like one candy bar cost $2 so two candy bars of the same brand, should cost $4. And the child's perspective of such is therefore justified to their self as true.

Truth is not only in types that would ignore what grants us a truth, which is appraisal. Therefore I offer the following, "Anything that we can conceive of in our mind and speak of then exists". This is true and cannot be otherwise, yet after you have read that first sentence, and to prove me wrong, you have likely thought up an abstract contradictory concept, perhaps a talking rabbit or the sun rising at night in the darkness. If you have not done so then I implore that you take a moment and do so...

Now with your attention returned and your fresh thought you can ask how your abstraction, let's say the talking rabbit, possibly exist. You may say that rabbits do not have the vocal cords to speak and a rabbit saying words, as we understand them, has not been recorded at any time in history. Since we are at that point I can show you how!

First Bugs Bunny is a rabbit, and that we can say is an objective truth; secondly, Bugs Bunny can talk, another objective truth; and third is the synthesis – Bugs Bunny is a rabbit that can talk. From this we can conclude that a talking rabbit does exist.

What absurd reasoning you may now say, but how would you argue your point. Is Bugs Bunny not real, does he not exist, is he not tangible; but you cannot argue by these means, for Bugs Bunny does exist or we would not be able to speak of such a conception. We would not have a point of reference. What you can argue here is the degree to which your conception exists and that degree which it has relevance to being a thing-unambiguous and not a concept-ambiguous.

The gradations in the degree of existence we can call truth values, and from these values we can begin to see how we perceive a concept per pounded as false, possible, or true. Once we have the value we can then say a concept is true objectively, subjectively, scientifically, and or mathematically, or false in those same arrangements. These arrangements are the definitive notions of the concept.

Truth value is an easy thing to consider. It is basically asking the question of how true something seems to me and often how apropos that something is to a situation. So to re-examine the talking rabbit simile; if we are speaking of a born and breathing, flesh adorned rabbit then of course it is false to say that there are talking rabbits and only true to say that talking rabbits exist only in fiction, like Bugs Bunny. As much as for something to *be so*, for something to *not be so* it must *be so* in some form; there must always be a *be so*.

Truth value judges a model of concepts. A concept is that which we derive from an individual experience and a concept is definitive by its nature – that is how it reacts to things external to it, and how things external react in turn. Everything that contributes to a concept contributes to its nature and thus must be as vulnerable as the concept.

Experiences cannot be false, they can only be or not be as they are the result of an unconscious occurrence that does not the possess the ability to do other than what it does; a person, however, can misinterpret by an error in cognition, so in that sense one can perceive an experience falsely thus having a false experience. For that to be the case they would still have a model of concepts of what they experienced which would then be judged true, possible, or false. The model of concepts is contained in what the model proposes.
A model could propose, after seeing a thing, "I have seen a tree". And the "I have seen a tree" would be what is scrutinized not the seeing of the thing; and one would have to be able to answer, did you see a tree (truth), or did you think you saw a tree (possibility), or were you seeing a light-post (falseness).

True, Possible, and False are ostensibly all of the truth values. That which is in between, Possible, has its own range of values, which determine how or perhaps why we are inclined to accept a thing as true or false and at some point change our mind. More than that true is expressed in separate values that allow us to judge a concept as true yet from a different standard.

From the lowest value we consider things false, and that which we call untrue and or a lie are not at the value level of being false. First, a lie represents intent to deceive, and with this intent will likely be represented from one person to another with the greatest possible truth value, so though it may indeed be false it will represent a truth. Secondly, an untruth is or should be understood as *not truth*, or in other words less than true, which means that it is still possible. Further still, it is not a lie if one is mistaken, erroneous, or ignorant. Ask yourself how many times you have considered a thing untrue until you were shown a proof, (and) then changed your mind to say that a thing was true or affirmed as false.

Falseness is a null value. A null value is that which we consider as having no value and not existing as constructed. The conviction which one has in a concept not having value is strong enough that it will not be a reversible consideration. It is then reserved for concepts with absurd constructions and could be quantified as by the number zero. My telling you that there is a talking rabbit, for instance, this concept is absurd so you assigned it no value, it has no possibility or credibility and it has no connection to an experience.

Perhaps due to naïveté or some form of cupidity, or a consideration of the person offering the concept, one can perceive a concept as being possible thus having affirmative value. Affirmative value is regarding a concept as having value, in the positive sense, and existing yet possibly conceived incorrectly – untrue. All value that is not null value possess affirmative value, in that affirmative value could be quantified by greater than zero (>0).

From the greater than zero affirmative value we can move closer to a concept being true with two more possibility values. Diminutive value is next; it is regarding a concept as having enough value to not just be considered, but to actually be positively considered as a truth and not likely to be false. Or in a way of being true with flaws, or true enough as much as one wishes to think of it. Next we have instrumental value. This is a value in which we consider a concept as having enough value to be shown as being true. It has the value that says, show me by a method or formula and I will accept the conclusion.

The next greatest values are those in which we no longer consider a thing as simply being possible but actually being true. The first truth is informative value, which is regarding a concept as being proven true based on contingencies with no less than instrumental value. That is it is proven true by proofs. The second truth, which is only a different form rather than a higher value, is unfalsifiable value, and this is when a concept is true by self evidence- i.e. the sun exists or I exist.

Unfalsifiability, though many examples of it can be offered, is a difficult value as it exists. In the same way an absurd concept is false, if one can say that if you can not disprove a concept than it is as real as a concept that can be proved in the informative value. For instance is the deist view of God, which is the God who is a kid with an ant hill, and disinterested with earth and indeed unable to do anything in human affairs.

One who seeks to refute a God theory does so by countering the religious conception, thereby falsifying proofs. And if there are no proofs as such, a concept can not be falsified as they permit no tests to evaluate their proofs. So one could say to a religious person that there is no God because there are no miracles, but to a deist the refutation of, "there is a God because there is a God", can only be there is not a God because there is not a God. Unfalsifiability though a value, is a flimsy value because it leaves open the possibility of an incorrect truth, in other words a contradiction. In an unfalsifiable concept, any scenario that it can create could be equally valid. Unfalsifiability is the equivalent of blind faith.

A problem is thus presented when unfalsifiability is scrutinized by the standard of non-contradiction, which is integral to a thing having affirmative value. A concept cannot be by nature contradictory and true. If two contrary natures are aroused in the same concept they negate each other and something will need to occur to create a change either in both of them or in one, until they no longer contradict.

Of course there too is difficulty in applying non-contradiction. For something to be judged by this standard the natures in question cannot have both the absence and presence of the same fixed quality, overlapping qualities. An overlapping quality means that two natures have fundamental differences, which further means that they can complement each other.

For instance, a meal of cereal and toast is commonly known as breakfast, and breakfast is understood as being eaten in the morning, whereas dinner is eaten in the evening. Because these events occur when they do, they can always retain their title. Thus is it contradictory to eat cereal and toast in the evening and call it dinner? Of course not, an overlapping nature is contained in each other, dinner is a meal at a time, and breakfast is a meal at a time.

The overlapping of "meal at a time" allows one to eat breakfast for dinner. Contradictions must be functional opposites, those natures which cannot exist in the same space and time, i.e. wet and dry, liquid and solid, or top and bottom. One of the two natures existing would negate the entire nature of the other.

Contradictions are not the greatest threat to truth value, because before we even approach a model to value we could create a poor concept. When constructing a concept we make a cognitive recognition of the sensory perception of an experience. An experience itself can only occur, however, if we misinterpret our sensory perception we can convert an experience into something other than what it was.

The result is a wrong concept, a bad model, and finally a truth with null value. Misinterpreted experiences are the result of errors in cognition, those are incorrect understandings. Errors in cognition are represented in two separate types.

Error one, of a contradictory nature, is the false positive, or believing deception, and error two is the false negative, or dismissing construction. In making a cognitive error, our minds are primed by our senses to prepare to interpret sensory information according to an expected connection. And for the type one error we interpret something as being so when it is not by creating a connection that does not exist.

For example, one regularly falls asleep at 9pm and typically awakes to an alarm clock, and sunlight at 6am; however, today they fall asleep with a lamp on, and their alarm malfunctions, waking the person at 3am. The person, use to the pattern of light and alarm, makes the incorrect connection that they should begin their day. They have made the mistake of believing in the deceiving appearance of light and sound and assume they are correct in rising for the day ahead. These false experiences led to the false concept, which resulted in the null value truth, as the person would at some point realize and return to their bed.

The error type two is the false negative, which is *not* believing something is so when it is, by not recognizing a connection. Here we return again to the sleeper, who has returned to sleep without re-setting his alarm clock, he is now asleep at 6am and his lamp too has been turned off. The sun light creeps in thru his window and lights up his room, he pulls the sheets over his face, and continues to sleep until 7am.

He failed to use the pattern of sun light and 6am, thereby dismissing the construction of his waking time with sunrise. His experience again was rendered false as he misinterpreted how light correlated to time and the false concept of what time it was which resulted in a null value truth of the model of morning. And once again once our sleeper realizes that value existence he will adjust, and rise to begin his day, late.

The patterns that we create have meaning to us, this is why we carry our false experience to null value truths before we realize that our experience was incorrectly interpreted; and some carry to affirmative value and lack the latter realization. Though we commit such cognitive errors, they persist as we continue to experience stimuli. This is likely due to a form of cost to benefit analysis that exists in our subconscious.

In a sense, whenever the cost of believing, in a false positive or false negative is less than the cost of not believing, and the potential benefit greater we will make such a cognitive error. Our sleeper had a greater benefit, in the first case; where it was better to be awake than to start the day late. And a higher cost in the second case where he considered that the cost of waking early meant more lost sleep whereas waking up at 6am or later was less important. We therefore make many incorrect connections to establish concepts that are more desirable or perhaps more necessary. A cognitive error thus could be better understood as staying with an error for lack of a better alternative.

A person knows the difference between the essence and integuments in the world yet their outlook bears more resemblance to cognitive errors. Truth then has the same value that a television drama has compared to real life. The assumption made is that integument is the essence of a concept, and that is the inevitable supposition. For example, to look at a statue and believe it is what it represents; that is like saying the Statue of Liberty *is* a large woman, rather than a large figure of a woman.

That would perhaps be a radical error, so to think more commonly, judging time on a broken clock. As the integument of what you have is a clock, thus a time measurement tool, if that is taken also as the essence of a broken clock, which is a time measurement tool that can not measure time, then one will not know the correct time.

To rescue ourselves from cognitive errors we must have counter concepts, or external constraints, that can be applied even to an integument that prevents its nature of falseness from predominating conception; and in this instance of clock, the external constraint is that a clock whose hands ho not move cannot count time. So in the least one confuses integument for essence and will at least not think it is perpetually 12 o'clock, and at some juncture realize that the clock is itself a broken clock.

Once one surpasses the error in cognition they can come to feel relieved and unable to return to the prior mode of understanding. The new truth after arrived at then is no longer compatible with the error, and more the conceiver would be discordant with others who persist in his old conception, as they would only be accustomed to think in integumental terms and he essential. The integumental thinkers are in a sense retaining an illusion, as the outer superstructure of a concept conveys a secondary impression to the nature of a concept as a representation of the concept. There indeed is a difference between a things outer layer – its integument – and what it does – its essence – and that difference illustrates different degrees in understanding and therefore truth.

For there to be truth there has to be the will to accept truth that follows the inclination to conclude truthful conceptions. This will to truth is the attempt to establish seemingly objective truths; as will to truth is making inferences from premise to conclusion. If the premise is true we would like the conclusion to be true, and the inverse. What derives from the will to truth is the will to deception, which has the affect of leading to a totalitarian ethic, because possessors of truth will want to impose their version of truth on others; if others perceive it as a fallacy then it is negated. Truth itself is akin to reason, if not derived from it, and what is reason; it is the faculty that calculates and decides, understands, and thinks before we commit an action.

Why do we make truth connections? What I mean is, why do we move a thought from premise to conclusion? This is because we are thinking animals; therefore we have to do so. It is unavoidable to think of a thought, they just occur to us, and as they occur we conclude them. We all therefore seek truth, not in any abstract sense, but for its own sake and because that is the only faculty we possess to that point. That truth is prior to will, and where the will takes over is in considering a conclusion itself true because we have a premise. When will is put forth one cannot help but feel the approach of negative motivations. This is only the case in one sense. The will to truth is mostly the faculty to conclude – finish the thought.

The pernicious will to truth is the faculty to deceive, which is what we commonly call a lie. The faculty to deceive is secondary to the will to truth; it arises after the natural premise to conclusive movement. Deception is the logical necessitation of an object which is inclined to a subject, or in other words a lie is someone trying to gain something which itself is an object or situation. Furthermore, and unlike truth, there is no deception for the sake of deception because the inclination towards truth is always the natural condition; deception is the artificial condition created ipso facto.

There is a form of truth that only presents a conundrum as derived from the will to truth, and that form is the contrary hypothetical. A contrary hypothetical is when a source gives you an affirmation that relies on the contingency given by a second source and the source gives a contingency that relies on the affirmation from the first source. There then is no true premise to move to a conclusion, only a premise that moves to another premise. Neither source is simpatico with the other, so neither can answer a question, though they can bring one closer to an answer, until there is a union of sources. And because a union of sources is unlikely, one can use one or the other contingency as their answer and likely the answer to their own advantage.

Contrary hypotheticals are truths in pieces. Let us say that the sources are two parents and the one is their child. The child first asks his or her mother or father for extra playtime and that parent responds, "ask your other parent and if they say yes than it is ok". The child goes to the second parent, and that parent says, "you can do it if your mother or father said you can". In this case the child has the affirmative, "yes it is ok", based on the contingency, "if your other parent says yes", and then the contingency, "if your mother or father says you can", then finally the reverse affirmative, "you can do it". Does the child then have permission? Yes and no.

If the child wants the object of their desire more than the true answer then they can connect the affirmatives, "yes it is ok...you can do it", indeed these were both offered to the child, so it is true. If the child prefers the truth as primary then they can bridge the sources by informing the parent of what the other said, in other words connecting a contingency with an affirmative for the source.

To break a contrary hypothetical is as simple as cross referencing sources. However, the aims of the subject will necessitate the results. If the subject favors its object then it will derive the truth that simply confers the object upon it. Truth indeed is what we make of it.

PART SEVEN
HOW ONE UNDERSTANDS THE WORLD

It is not vanity to say that the language we use for our system of classifications can ascribe contradictions to phenomena. Indeed, rhetoric has meaning, and when we classify a thing, we should not diminish the characteristics we thus apply by calling them clumsy concepts. The label of rationalist or the use of rationalism or the verb to rationalize, as a concept, has a common use, however, is oft misused in attempts to describe an unambiguous mode of conceptualization. The rationale of a concept is created by using any means of thought to connect strands of assumptions into a conceptualization. The concept could be at the utmost extent of absurdity or abstraction, however, if one can make it sensible to their self then it becomes hard to refute.

Rationalism is reductionism, or a form of it. To reduce complexity or ambiguity to simplicity has as one prominent quality, intentionality. Rationalism is an attempt at conclusiveness, because for a conclusion to be reached we have to accept that no further knowledge can be added to a concept. For conclusion there too must be intent. Therefore, rationalism is an intentional attempt to respond to a question with finality.

A rationalization, from the perspective of its creator, is not an attempt to reduce the concrete to the abstract; it is an attempt at the contrary, making the abstract concrete. The better strategy for recognition of the abstract is the full compilation of the determinants in a concept, or pre fixed assumptions, identifying them as exigent parts and applying them to the succession of parts. Thus like a mechanical canard it will digest successfully with all parts adjoined.

If one dismisses familiar assumption then the beginning of knowledge is obscured, and rationalism is the only process remaining to consider a principle. The possession of all relevant information, knowledge of available methods, and a system of logical discernment – experimentation – are the optimum conditions of knowledge. These stanzas cannot, however, be enacted without the original assumptions.

The disparate, incomplete, and frequently contradictory assumptions are possessed separately by individuals. If an individual's assumption is dismissed and or excluded from the process of creating knowledge, then the individual is left with rationalism as their only mechanism of confirmation. Knowledge arrived at in this instance would have to be regarded as subjective knowledge, even if the assumption was likely to be rejected. It is subjective because a contradictory concept can be formed, legitimized, and presented from the existing assumption, after that assumption is rationalized into a logical concept.

Three methods must be highlighted in the methodology of rationalism: first, arguing from actualization, or artificial superstructure, second,

131

arguing from acuteness, or brevity in structure, and third, arguing from extrinsicality, or circumstantialities in structure. In actualization everything presenting itself as different is reduced to identity as the artificial concealment of something else or the manifestation of something intransigent.

With extrinsicality a category or classification may not be reducible to the central identities of a prescribed form; in this case its relation to the fundamental principle desired allows it to be bypassed for a dialectical synthesis of relatable concepts, and therefore identity is systematically reified. For the argument from acuteness a brief succession of stages perpetuates a concentration of abstractions from an approximation to a paradigm. All methods have the same realization in mind, a pseudo answer.

When one makes an attempt to convert an assumption into rationalism and their attempts take the form of arguing from extrinsicality, then one is forming an argument with circumstantial structure. The extrinsic argument is the form of rationalism with the greatest form of intentionality. it is an attempt to subvert a category or classification when it does not fit a central postulate. The original concepts relation to the desired principle allows it to be bypassed in favor of a dialectical synthesis of a relatable concept. The concepts identity is thus systematically reified and presented as something different.

Extrinsicality is inadequate as a form of argument, and I offer the following example to highlight its speciousness. An old man points to a twenty year old gentleman and asks him, "do you or do you not have a beard". The gentleman replies, "I have one", and the inquisitor responds, "how can you say you do, with only strands and patches of hair"? The young man retorts, "I can say I have a beard because I have the beginnings of one, I have a quantity of individual hairs on my face, and a beard is a quantity of individual hairs".

The young gentleman is obviously being specious as he, being a man and young, desires the full status of being a man of age, which comes with having a beard; a condition that most virile young men find themselves in. He extrinsically rationalizes a beard, for he does not have one, he has facial hair growing into a beard, it is therefore becoming a beard.

With extrinsic rationalism one purposefully manipulates an outcome by adjusting circumstances. As we see in the example, the circumstances the young man applies to the nature of a beard are manipulated to fit the young man's present situation. This alters both what the young man has as well as the logical concept; that is to say the nature of a beard itself. The obvious synthesis in this case is that a person with a beard has facial hair, and a person with no facial hair has no beard. Therefore, a person with some facial hair has a beard.

An extrinsic rationalism is not complete falseness; it is at the same time not an objective truth. The confusion comes from the method, which has as one of its qualities intentionality. More than any other form of rationalism, extrinsicality is an implicit attempt at a forced conclusion.

Not just an attempt at a conclusion, but one in the favor of the person who created the rationalism. This argument is almost antithetical to the argument from actualization, where truth or even speciousness is not considerations. Actualization creates circumstances, and is limited in that regard.

The argument from acuteness is a postulate from apathy, or a like sentiment. One is too disconnected, disinterested, or unaffected by the outcome of their conclusion that they prefer the simplest evaluation of their assumption. In creating a lethargic conclusion they are not, however, disinterested in the rightness of their conclusion, only its creation. The lack of interest also corresponds to a lack of intent and in this sense we can say that the argument from acuteness is significantly different than to the argument from extrinsicality where one purposefully manipulates an outcome.

The difficulty with this argument is in its refutation. If the rationalist is not particularly interested in it and uses the most spurious reasoning then they will be equally disinterested in defending their rationalism. The new rationalism is accepted as true, and once a predatory person realizes this, they will accept the rationalism as no less then useful. Once again we return to extrinsicality, only this time it is sympathetic to acuteness. Indeed once an acute rationalism progresses from personal idiosyncrasy to public consumption, to possession, it requires further justification.

The acute rationalism is a concentration of abstractions, creating a paradigm from an approximation. Though acuteness embraces multiple abstractions, its multiplicity is not the multiplicity of assumptions prior to knowledge. It would take an immense amount of reduction to make an assumption as plain as possible; therefore an assumption is an amalgam of abstractions. Furthermore, using the label of acuteness is meant to imply a method that uses the least, and narrowest amount of content.

Acute rationalism does this by approximating the abstractions within an assumption. That is to say it does not consider any abstraction as valid, invalid, contradictory, or useless, simply as parts of a whole. When one acutely rationalizes the action is so brief that the abstractions are not consciously conceived, and it is more as if the abstractions are accepted. The only consideration given is to the assumption. The acute rationalism is in the same format as its original assumption.

An assumption contains abstractions, and the assumptions that are included prior to knowledge are submitted from their own process of knowledge. If an assumption contains contradictory aspects then one aspect has to be reasoned out for the assumption to survive as a contingency prior to knowledge. Acute rationalism says that some aspects will remain contradictory and does not attempt to correct these differences. The only thing that is important in this method of argument is that a question is assigned an answer.

The final rationalized concept may have significant holes and a flimsy premise; however, its lack of depth does not prevent it from being usable. Rather than collapsing, the acute rationalism is malleably applied to other conditions. Since the contradictions have not been vetted one can use one of any to show a line of construction that conforms to a viewpoint. Outlying pieces are always menacing in this way.

Reductionism can also be applied to an acute rationalism to attempt to mask it as knowledge, however incomplete, by showing the contingent abstractions, not as abstractions, but contingent assumptions. Acute rationalism cannot withstand scrutiny as it comes in contact with reality it eventually manifests errors. It thus takes extrinsicality to bypass a fact and continue to argue.

Another form of rationalism, and not one considered an argument from a rationalist perspective, is relativity. It is not considered an argument in and of itself because it is a sub-argument of acuteness. Thinking relatively is thinking shortly. To think in that way means, quite simply, to think of the final concept in terms of how its contingent parts relate to each other, and base their relationship on how they relate to an equal third part.

Using mathematical formulae, relativity is when a first variable equals a second variable, the second variable equals a third variable, and from this we derive the conclusion that the first variable is equal to the third. The mathematical characterization does not fully underscore the nature of a relativistic conclusion. One is not typically considering a mathematical nature when making this connection and the variables being compared may not have any common equivalence between them, and typical of rationalism, all assumptions are not part of the process.

Let us consider a most common use of relative rationalism, athletic competition. It is late in the season and the big game is looming between two unbeaten teams, gamblers, speculators, and sports media alike, all wanting to know for whatever reason, the outcome before the game.

So they compare statistics, which do not lead to any real satisfaction, as stats are relative to the manner in which a particular team chooses to play a game and do not fully underscore the competitor's quality. The only thing left to turn to is common opponents, and say, team A will play team B, they both played team C. Team A defeated team C by 2 points and team B defeated team C by 20 points.

And with other factors put aside, team A will defeat team B. Yet any casual sports fan will tell you, though they have likely made this calculation themselves, it hardly bears out. Relativism is too narrow to, itself, be a predictor of an outcome.

In the form of arguing from actualization, rationalism superimposes an artificial superstructure over a concept in the place of understanding. Actualization does not seek differentiation in any number of concepts; it is an argument to reduce complexity. The argument reduces one thing to something else. That is to say that in the argument from actualization, one rationalizes the nations of Asia as being eastern nations, because they are east in sailing from Europe and around the cape of South Africa.

The creation of an artificial superstructure is both the first and the most important part of arguing from actualization. To bring an argument to conclusion in this vain one must first create the conditions by which the original assumption is defined. This is not the same as acuteness, which amalgamates the abstractions that create the assumption or extrinsicality which uses existing circumstances and manipulates them.

Actualization is a creator, and the most involved of the three arguments. To create the artificial superstructure of my 'Asia to the east' example one must conceive as such: (1) the earth, which is a sphere, is looked at on a flat surface (2) the Atlantic ocean is the middle of the earth (3) east is to the right hand side, west to the left (4) taking Europe and Asia together, being on the same land mass, Europe is to the left of Asia. Using these four conditions of the structure of the world map I can rationalize, or conclude, that Asia is to the east.

One can easily make the counter argument; if they place the Pacific Ocean at the center of the world, and proportion the map correctly, Asia will be to the left or west, with Europe to the right or East. Both manners of thinking are artificial, and can be further refuted when you consider global position from the reality that earth is a sphere that rotates perpetually and or that Asia and Europe are on the same land mass to the east, or west of the Americas. It would be much equally artificial to say that Europe-Asia is to the north of Africa and Australia.

Artificial structure defines the entire premise of arguing from actualization. As one reduces everything to an identity, to manifest an intransigent concept, what they are doing is establishing the contingent pieces of the artificial structure. Therefore, everything revolves around that structure. And this structure, though comprising pieces, is not complex, it is simple.

It is simple because it does not gather assumptions; instead it gathers completed knowledge to pose that as an answer to its central assumption. Instead of counterpoising its assumption with other assumptions, therefore trending towards knowledge, it accepts its assumption as nearly fully correct. The artificial structure is thus retroactively imposed.

The final rationalism that comes from actualization is superfluous. As was shown by my Asian example, one only needs to change the structure and the concept collapses. This is not only the endemic problem with actualized rationalism; the weakness of arguments is the problem with rationalism in general and the reason to question its use.

The use of rationalism is relative to reductionism, in that they seek a means to an end in regards to a logical concept or an understanding. The methods of both do differ but the ends seem to derive from the same reasoning, an explanation as one understands it or can understand it for their own purposes. In reductionism one looks for the understanding of the nature of complexities by reducing them to the interactions of their contingencies or the sum of their parts or more fundamental or simpler things.

We see the main difference of rationalism and reductionism in the direction of the inclination. Rationalism is building up to a conclusion from a contingency or assumption, whereas reductionism is as its name suggests, beginning from a conclusion or concept and stepping it backward, with the goal of understanding its parts. Where these two systems converge is in that they are equally laissez-fair, casual, and lethargic approaches to outcomes.

The two methods of discernment have, even in their key differences, fundamental similarity. Where I see the main divergence is in the use of the terminology itself. Where rationalist is generally accepted as having a positive connotation, reductionist is a label often applied after one has come to a conclusion, and an observer views it as unfavorable to their position. It would seem that using reductionist is the same lampoon as labeling a person a simpleton.

When an atheist, for example, uses the argument against the existence of a creator god they typically say, if there is this thing that created everything then what created the creator. And rather than respond, because there is no logical response to such a tautology, the atheist is labeled reductionist, and thus one who overlooks the complexity, of the being in question.

When reductionism seeks to explain, it looks at the parts of a concept, as being the concepts defining qualities. Therefore, and in this instance excluding a mechanical construct, a logical concept is defined by its assumptions, but not by the collection of relevant information, knowledge of available methods of and the system of discernment. Mechanical constructs, on the other hand, have literal parts that are used to build the machine. In using an analogy that applies to both, is it realistic to define a car by its tires, and windshield, and mirrors, etc. Or is it more definitive to say that a car is a vehicle, and then define the qualities of a vehicle?

Reductionism is not the best way to define a thing. However, it is a reasonable way to contemplate a thing, for is not a car the sum of its tires, and windshield, and mirrors, etc. Indeed it is; however, that manner of conception does not allow you the unambiguous knowledge of what constitutes a car, and not just what it is but how it functions, and what differentiates it from a truck.

Rationalism in a contrary sense would make the same mistake of not allowing one to perceive the quality of what makes a car, as we know it, a car. When I refer to a car, one realizes what I am referencing to, it is *a priori* knowledge. What if this car only had ten inch wheels, and was powered by AA batteries? I can still say that this car has wheels, a windshield, mirrors, etc. However this is not the car we would typically reference. This is a toy.

For me to call this a car, I have to perceive its parts and rationalize that the item constructed with the parts, postulated in the reductionist definition of a car, do indeed constitute a car. Rationalism builds from the contingent parts to construct a conclusion.

Reductionism seeks to simplify complexity by previewing the parts, as the definitive whole. Rationalism wants to make sense of the complex, and is secondary to reductionism, in that it constructs a conclusion from the scattered parts. Each is a method that does not seem to derive from the desire to understand, rather the desire to conclude.

Describing rationalism as a method is an attempt to differentiate what is inherently different in knowledge, and that is process. Knowledge itself exists in a multiplicity of ways, knowing how a concept works or complex knowledge, or knowing that which a concept entails or common knowledge, are the usages of my chief concern. These are the depths of knowledge that require the process of knowing or learning and experiencing.

The others types of knowledge, knowing of persons, of places, and of actions, are associated with acquaintanceship with such things. One can not rationalize an acquaintance or literal experience, only in the sense that they describe the same thing that another perceives via the same physical sensations of, touch, taste, sight, smell, and or sound, in different rhetorical terms. For that case we would only be arguing semantics, or to take a Shakespearean example, "a rose by any other name is still a rose".

Knowledge by process begins similar to rationalism, with an assumption. The next progression, and where they begin the divergence, is the collection of assumptions; that is if there is more than one to collect. With knowledge, if there are multiple assumptions, then each is part of the original consideration, and acts upon each other assumption to inform their formation in conceptualization.

Rationalism on the other hand begins and ends with a singular assumption. There can be knowledge that begins with a single assumption; it is the entire process though that determines the classification of the outcome. Furthermore, it is knowledge associated with acquaintanceship, or a priori, where we typically see singular assumptions.

Beyond this as well, knowledge with a singular assumption is incredibly rare, and is usually secondary knowledge – knowledge as the result of an already established understanding; meaning I have seen a picture of a mountain, and read the definition of a mountain, and am aware of things with names such as Mount Olympus, thus when I see one in person I have one assumption of what it might be.

The process of knowledge in this instance would be very brief, as it would be knowledge acting upon knowledge, and verify that what I am looking at is most likely a mountain. What this instance does highlight is the second progression of knowledge, and its divergence with rationalism. In knowledge one collects all relevant information.

My latter example does not fully highlight this part of knowledge, because all relevant information includes information that is different or contradictory. Thus I must also have pictures of other earth formations, gorges, plateaus, and especially hills, as part of my formation of the concept of what constitutes a mountain. I must also understand the definition of gorge, plateau, and hill, and must be aware of things like The Grand Canyon, Columbia Plateau, and Bunker Hill – or my uneven rear yard – to make the full comparison, and say that when I see a mountain it is indeed a mountain, and not one of the other three.

This example is limited, because for acquaintanceship the next two progressions of knowledge are either parts of the second part, or superfluous in there meaning. For the latter progressions I will use the most common mathematical platitude, which is the addition of one and one equaling two. The final two progressions of knowledge exist as mutually exclusive fashions that bring us back to the knowledge that I prefer to highlight; knowledge of how something works or complex knowledge, and knowledge of what a concept entails or common knowledge. The last two progressions are, first, awareness of available methods, and finally, a system of logical discernment.

To exemplify the entire process I will begin my banal mathematical expression at the beginning of the knowledge process, and then return for a brief differentiation of the complex and common knowledge. I only write this because, all of this knowledge will seem common to the reader and a digression will be needed.

To begin with, I have the available assumptions: 1. I have one thing, let us use an apple for clarity, and I have another apple 2. These are not the same object, as my *a priori* knowledge of things has discerned 3. I possess these apples, it is assumed that my knowledge of *how* I possessed them already exists 4. There are more than one apple, it is assumed that I already know the concept of one 5. With these apples put together I possess a different number of apples.

With all of these assumptions taken together, and barring any outlying assumptions that I have overlooked my knowledge progresses to the next stage. I collect all relevant information, and in this instance the relevant information is that I possess one apple and one other apple. In the next progression I conceive all the methods that will illuminate what I have, and in this case, I can count numbers, and equate the number I count with the number of apples or I can use the mathematical formula of addition, and add my one apple to the other apple and create a group of apples.

If I choose my system of logical discernment as addition, then I say, in math when I add the number one, to the number one I have the number two, thus I have two apples. Once I conceive the completion of the process, then my resulting knowledge is, the number one corresponds to an apple, and I have added a one and a one to make two, thus an apple and another apple is two apples. Thus you have the process of knowledge.

Of course the process is typically more rapid, especially in cases where the logical discernment is using a calculation, and where *a priori* knowledge assists in the process. The two knowledge differences however still require a highlight. The pre-existing knowledge and the knowledge that can activate rapidly is the common knowledge. Although I drew out the process of knowing that I have two apples above, it does not take very long to know this, and one does not consider the logical discernment.

One simply knows that adding one to one will give them two. The complex knowledge actually knows how to add one to one, and as I also mentioned in the example, I could have counted to from one to two which is using a common knowledge method. This would not have been the task of using a mathematical formula. If I had fifty bushels of apples I would have to use a mathematical formula to count them if I want an accurate and timely count, and to know how to use the formula I would need to use complex knowledge.

Not dissimilar to knowledge, the act of rationalizing an assumption is not the act of passive conceptualization. For one to reduce a concept to its less ambiguous form, in other words to respond to a postulate, one has to act with purpose. And the only purpose behind bypassing the process of knowledge in lieu of the method of rationalism is a level of several factors, apathy, lethargy, and or lack of relevance. Rationalism is to active a process for it to not be the result of intentionality when one comes to a rationalized conclusion. If a person simply looks at a tree and wonders why the leaves are green, if they do not want an answer they will not conceive one. For them to answer the question, they must intentionally pursue the visages of photosynthesis. Otherwise they just understand the tree as being green rather than why.

Intentionality is a mental phenomenon as is rationalism. And for mental phenomena there must first be an object, and then content. In this case rationalism is the object and intentionality is its content. This juxtaposition is of course not always the case. As an object rationalism can be realized with a disparate multitude of content and intentionality can be the content of other objects or an object in and of itself. Content is directed towards another object, and is not the justification of the original object, it is its method. That is to say for the object of "thinking" there is the content of "thought", and thought exists to think about objects other than its self. Intentional rationalism seeks to rationalize, and not to rationalize intent.

Mental phenomenon outside of this phenomenological construct is subject to its actions, therefore, any object or content can be rationalized. And although it is called a mental phenomenon it does not imply randomness only that it occurs in the mind, without clarity of a clear reason for why it occurs in the mind.

There are objects that exist in the understanding and objects that exist in reality. Objects that exist in understanding are those of the mental phenomena and are indifferent to physical phenomena. Physical phenomena can neither be explained in the same way as mental phenomena, nor do they necessarily react upon each other.

Objects that exist in understanding have to be confirmed; however, the confirmation can be done with a rationalization. An object does not have to be real to be understandable; it only has to be conceivable.

Take for example a transatlantic bridge, no such piece of architecture exists, and will not likely be planned or attempted. However, I can construct in my mind what such a thing would look like, and how it would function. For an object to exist in reality, and here I replace that phrase with the word objective, it has to meet the standard of proof that is the process of knowledge.

Therefore, for my bridge to exist objectively, someone needs to, at least, start drawing up the blueprints. This is where the mental phenomena of intentional rationalism occur. The objects of understanding and the mental phenomena are not dissimilar to assumptions. I assume a bridge can be built.

It is not difficult to see from my example how intentionally rationalizing a transatlantic bridge as having a lack of relevance to myself. I am not an architect, and such an undertaking may have no practical application, and therefore I also have apathy as my connection to this assumption. I did, though, have to form the thought for it to exist, and I might add in a context that did not inspire the thought. One simply does not accidentally come to a rationalization without meaning to do it.

I can ask myself this question, is the sky blue because the water is blue, or is the water blue because the sky is blue? I do not know the answer to either question, and for the purpose of making my argument I will not attempt to find out until I complete this work. Therefore, I will rely on a rationalism to answer this question. What I also fail to consider is that both or neither may be the case, and their colors may be mutually exclusive. What I truly have in my purview is whether rationalism has the affect of abstracting the concrete or of elucidating the abstract or of doing both.

It would seem that rationalism has the affect of abstracting that which is concrete because it prevents the full establishment of knowledge and contributes to the denigration of established knowledge. The water is blue because the sky is blue. Any cup of water that I have ever filled has been fully translucent, and has no less than the color of the cup that contains it. The greater the amount of water, it seems, the more or deeper the mimicry of color.

I have seen blue looking water and white looking water in private pools. Shallow puddles seem to have the color of the pavement or dirt that they cover. As I have rationalized this acutely, I have no concern or interest in my being right. Furthermore, I was lethargic in constructing this argument, as I have no contributory knowledge. I simply see what is abstract, that blueness occurs in clear water. It is and there are, knowledge of and ways for me to review and add to my knowledge, the reason behind the blue color. Because I have not done so, I have reduced the value of the knowledge, by accepting my own conclusion, thus abstracting the concrete.

There is the possibility, and indeed the greater locus of experience, of using rationalism to do the obverse and cement the abstract. I am re-appropriating the word abstract, and in this sense instead of using it to define the contingencies of an assumption, I am using its meaning as anything lacking clear understanding. That encompasses abstractions before assumptions, assumptions themselves, and concepts that do not inspire assumptions. I must therefore ask a question as my assumption.

Is the sky blue because the water is blue? It would, based on another acute rationalism, seem to be the case. I base this on no process of reasoning, only this: the oceans are blue at any time of day and the sky changes color from many external obstructions; the sky must be, to some extent reflective; with the ocean the largest, colored feature, the sky reflects their color.

The condition that makes this an elucidated conclusion, whereas the latter was not, is the condition of it being an open ended conclusion. This conclusion can be advanced or reapplied due to its having only one contingency that is closed, the color of the water. Open ended conclusions are needed to make something clearer if one accepts that rationalism is not final knowledge.

There is an overriding principle that binds not only the methods of rationalism, but also the process of knowledge. This raison d'être is conclusiveness. There is, though, a difference between an objective conclusion and rational conclusiveness.

This latter form of conclusion is the result of an intentional method; whereas knowledge is indifferent to its own conclusion, because it cannot control the result due to its process. Rationalism is precisely the construct for a desired result. People will create illusions when they have nothing else to hold on to; and with knowledge typically being out of reach and difficult to grasp one rationalizes to have nothing less than a foundation to stand on top of.

Why the mind desires conclusiveness from all arenas I am not prepared to answer here. That the mind desires conclusion, I can rationalize as being so. It is the same as saying that man is curious and wants to satisfy that curiosity, thus providing the rationale for exploration in all fields. However, exploration of an assumption is not always possible.

If I was a medieval Venetian merchant, say, who heard of this magnificently wealthy land of Mexico and the New World and could not afford a galleon to make the voyage, I would have to satisfy myself with maps and stories, as confirmation that this place existed.

From these maps and stories I could make an acute rationalism, as the facts would not matter because I could never make the journey. However, I would be satisfied that I supposedly know that this place exists. You may not fully see how this example is a rationalized conclusion, because it is now objectively true that there is a Mexico and the New World of the Americas. Perhaps a more contemporary consideration is needed. The search for the earth like planet is more modern, and based on the rational conclusion that the conditions for life exist in this galaxy, and there are countless galaxies, therefore there should be the conditions for life elsewhere.

In that sense I must concede that rational conclusiveness is indeed necessary. Though I can only maintain this concession for open ended conclusions, or put differently, conclusions that are made with the intent to arrive at other conclusions. Knowledge or logical conclusion is an attempt to arrive at a conclusion that is proved by the process of creating knowledge. The logical conclusion is intended only as a conclusion in and of its self. The rational conclusion is a conclusion of and for itself – or its creator, I.